To: Kim Pagano

Dear Kim,
    Thank you so very much for your interest, I am looking forward to talking to you next week. May God continue to

Till the End of Time

Richly bless you and all y... ...ved ones.
    With all my lov
    Sylvia Anthony

By
Sylvia Anthony

Sylvia's Haven
A Story of Persistence, Love, Failure, and Success in a Woman's Life

www.xulonpress.com

THE WHITE HOUSE

WASHINGTON

November 27, 2002

Ms. Sylvia Anthony
Post Office Box 2163
Ayers, Massachusetts 01432-2163

Dear Ms. Anthony:

I am pleased to send warm greetings and congratulations on being named a Daily Point of Light. This recognition pays tribute to your important efforts to lend a helping hand to others.

Every day in our great Nation, outstanding individuals make a positive difference in their communities. I commend you for upholding this proud tradition through your volunteer service to your fellow citizens. Your hard work and dedication enhance the quality of life for others and demonstrate the caring and generous spirit that makes our country strong.

Laura joins me in sending best wishes on this special and memorable occasion.

Sincerely,

George W. Bush

AMBASSADOR FOR PEACE

The Interreligious and International Federation for World Peace

Consistent with its mission to establish world peace, the Interreligious and International Federation for World Peace acknowledges as Ambassador for Peace those individuals whose lives exemplify the ideal of living for the sake of others, and who dedicate themselves to practices which promote the founding ideals of the IIFWP: universal moral values, strong family life, interreligious cooperation, international harmony, renewal of the United Nations, a responsible public media, and the establishment of a culture of peace. Transcending racial, national and religious barriers, the Ambassadors for Peace contribute to the fulfillment of the hope of all ages, a unified world of peace wherein the spiritual and material dimensions of life are harmonized.

The Interreligious and International Federation for World Peace
is proud to hereby recognize as an Ambassador for Peace,

Mrs. Sylvia Anthony

Rev. Dr. Sun Myung Moon, Founder

Dr. Hak Ja Han Moon, Co-Founder

Acknowledgments

I want to forever thank God for His wisdom, endless guidance, boundless love, and miraculous help in the creation of this story, and my creation. Without Him it would never have unfolded as it has.

I will be forever grateful for the love given to me by my Grandparents and Uncles. Without them this story could not be told.

I wish to thank John Griffiths who assisted me in this endeavor. John was an enormous help with his typing, editing, adding, and deleting as he and I thought fit, on the original manuscript, "Sylvia's Haven." "Till the End of Time," is the revised version of "Sylvia's Haven" that has been brought up to date to this current year.

To Jim Holmes, my assistant who worked for hours and hours to transfer the book "Sylvia's Haven" into this computer so that it could be revised and become "Till the End of Time."

I want to thank my Pastor Rick Picariello, for being so helpful in many ways, and the whole Picariello family. Pastor Brian Krough, and his wife Lori. To Steve Viola and family who have worked, hands on in so many ways. To Bill Sullivan, and his wife Karen, for having the grace to listen to my needs and pray and assist me, and to Joanne Murchie and Mary Basler for all of their assistance. I could go on and on, but my church has over 400 members. Therefore, I say to all the people of Mount Hope Church, thank you for being a second family to me.

To my sister, who I love dearly, my mother and father, and to all of my family, friends, staff, volunteers, and contributors, I give my enduring thanks, without them, I might never have had a chance to even try to accomplish God's grand design for this poor soul.

Sylvia Anthony

Table of Contents

A WORD FROM THE AUTHOR

I firmly believe God put me and each and every one of us on this earth for a specific reason, chosen by our creator.

As Woodrow Wilson stated:

"You are here to enrich the world. To live more amply, with greater vision, and with a finer spirit of hope and achievement."

When we do the right thing with the right motives, there is no limit as to how far we can go, with the help of God.

Our creator put everything on earth we need, to use or find use of. We will never stop learning from the day we are born, until the day we die. If we don't listen and use our minds in the direction it wants to go, and do nothing with it, it is a wasted life. It doesn't matter what the calling. The calling is different for each and every one of us.

As you read this book, you will see all the twists and turns my life has made. Every one of these experiences, bad or good, led me to where I am today.

From the day I was conceived it appeared to be a big mistake, but to God the timing was perfect. My parents did not want me. Therefore, He provided loving grandparents, uncles, and cousins who did.

My father was abusive, and in order to feel superior he belittled me and my mother continuously. At age five I lost my favorite, 18 year old uncle, through a drowning, and my grand uncle to cancer at age six.

In the bible it says, "Mourning may come for a night, but the new day will bring gladness." At age seven, I had a new baby sister, which I sorely needed at that point. The abuse at home only served to make me more determined to get out as fast as I could.

At eighteen, I married. This was not the answer. I found myself into another very bad situation. The only good thing it produced, were three children. A divorce ensued, after twelve and a half years. Now I had three children to support and a mortgage on the home we were living in. God provided a job that would pay the expenses. It was hard labor, but I had three children to raise and no choice in the matter.

After ten years, I married again. This was a good marriage. Now that my children were grown, God stepped in, and instilled in me the urge to have a shelter for homeless women and children, and the heart after all I had been through to understand their plight. It has now been nearly 25 years and 1060 women and children have been helped. At age eighty one, I still have the burning desire to help these women and children as never before, and will continue to do so until God takes me home.

My advice to you is never give up, whatever comes your way, it is all worth it.

Sylvia Anthony

Chapter 1

❧

Sylvia was born October 5, 1929, just about a week before the stock market crash and the beginning of the Great Depression. Both of her parents came from the same Sicilian town of Villarosa. Both sets of grandparents, lifelong friends, took slightly different paths to this country.

Her mother was brought to the U.S. in April of 1909, when she was only three months old, with the whole family. Her father came in 1924, when he was fourteen. In both cases, the grandfathers came without their extended families at first. There was a single goal always in mind: accumulate enough money to send for the rest of their families as soon as possible.

In her father's case, her paternal grandfather owned and operated a sulfur mine in Sicily. Sylvia's father was taken to work at the sulfur mine at age seven. This was not unusual in that time. All children were only given three years of schooling and were taught a crash course of reading, writing, and arithmetic. That was all the government offered at that time. Therefore, at age seven the children had completed their schooling.

Baby Sylvia in her mother's arms and her extended family

Sylvia's grandfather, was very successful, and his wife had household help. He also kept buying better equipment in order to get deeper into the earth, when the vane of sulfur disappeared, his debt to the equipment manufactures did not. Being a very honorable man, he left for America to make enough money to repay his creditors and, eventually send for his wife.

He took his oldest son, Sylvia's father, age fourteen at the time, with him. They could both work and reunite the family more quickly. When they arrived in America, they found the school system was quite different. Here, they insisted the boy go to school evenings. He was taught to speak English, and acquired more schooling. They examined him to see exactly where he would fit in the school system.

It was difficult for Chuck to comprehend what they were trying to teach him, but one subject became very understandable, that was mathematics. The numbering system was the same as in Italy and he could breeze through mathematics. With his knowledge of mathematics the school determined he had the equivalent of a seventh grade child in America.

Sylvia's father and grandfather eventually roomed in the home of Sylvia's maternal grandparents — the home, of course, of Sylvia's mother. Both grandfathers were very good friends and Jodie's father, (Sylvia's maternal grandfather) invited her paternal grandfather and son to come live with them. By this time, Chuck and his father had worked for five years in this country, and Chuck was now 19 years of age. This was quite a convenient matchmaking scenario for Sylvia's parents.

Jodie and Chuck not only lived in the same house together, they also worked in the same candy factory, in different departments, but they were able to be with each other at coffee breaks and lunch, where they ate their bagged lunches. The inevitable happened.

Her mother became pregnant. Her maternal grandfather became so enraged he threatened to kill her. He demanded that, she tell him who the father was. She told him, "It was Chuck." The fear of her father caused her mother to run away to New York City. She contacted the Traveler's Aid Society for assistance and, of course, the Society contacted her family.

Jodie's father told Chuck's father that his son was the father of the baby Jodie was carrying. Chuck's father demanded that Chuck go to New York and take Jodie back home and marry her. Chuck went to New York to retrieve her. Sylvia's parents were married on August 30, 1929, and took yet another room in the same house. In the meantime, Chuck's father sent for the rest of his family. They arrived in America on May 29, 1929. Sylvia joined them on October 5, 1929.

While her father had difficulty finding work, her mother, a very beautiful and intelligent woman, had no problem finding employment. When she found employment, she approached Chuck's Mother, informing her that she now was going to work and that she had to take care of Sylvia. She told Chuck's mother, "Here you take care of her, it was your son who got me in this mess." The grandmother gladly took her, she never did have a daughter of her own.

Sylvia's mother, Sylvia at thirteen, her father, and younger sister

In fact, the whole family welcomed Sylvia with open arms. She was the first girl in the family. Her mother worked in a factory making leather pouches. Her father continued to look for work, eventually taking an apprenticeship in a shoe-repair shop. He later purchased his own business to provide for the family.

During her childhood, Sylvia grew up in a very loving environment made by two sets of grandparents, a grand uncle, and four uncles. However, her parents considered her to be the cause of many of their own relationship problems. They did not treat Sylvia well. Father was extremely cruel and abusive and the mother simply ignored her.

Even as young as three, she felt that she had the wrong set of parents, in her own mind she felt these could not have been her real parents. Perhaps she was adopted?

Not only did her parents blame her for their problems, but also blamed each other all of their lives. This was a sin that stayed with them, and Sylvia was the scapegoat. It caused a great deal of strife, even violence. Her home was full of resentment. Her parents did not argue openly all the time, but these resentments hung like an ever-present dark cloud that would explode to violence every so often.

Some of Sylvia's earliest childhood memories remain vivid to this day. For example, she remembers how her grandmother would put her down for a nap in a very strange manner. Having to care for her own home, the grandmother scheduled Sylvia's nap time at ten in the morning, so that she could do her housework. She would put Sylvia on her lap and cover her face with a towel to keep out the light.

Rocking gently, she would say, rather loudly, "Nona, Nona." This went on until Sylvia went to sleep.

Sylvia, however, remembers thinking how odd it was. How did she expect to get her to sleep with such a racket going on? Now mind you Sylvia was only about five months old. She was too young to talk. Yet she was thinking in English.

Sylvia is positive, that the child's brain, and all other parts of the body begin to grow from the time of conception. A child may not know how to mouth the words immediately. But the learning process was in place. How else could she think to herself, in English.

Another instance: When Sylvia was about eighteen months old, her parents were returning home from work via different paths. Her mother got home first, and her father beat her for not having supper ready when he arrived. Even at that time, Sylvia remembers the incongruity of the timing and the awful viciousness of her father.

One uncle, Vincent, the second oldest of the four, was only thirteen years of age when Sylvia was born. As they got older, he learned to play the saxophone and clarinet and would teach a very young Sylvia many songs. She would sing along as he played.

When she was four, on one lovely summer's Saturday, Sylvia went outside. She then went down three doors from her home to a neighborhood school. There, on the steps, another older girl talked with her, eventually leaving. Oblivious to the time (it must have been at least 5:00 PM), Sylvia saw her uncle Salvy (Salvatore) walking very quickly on the other side of the street. She called out to him, "Salvy, where are you going?" He came over to her and exclaimed, "There you are, everyone has been looking all over for you. Your father is going to kill you."

They returned home, but by the time Sylvia neared the first-floor apartment, her father caught her in the hallway and started beating her unmercifully. Vincent, who was already inside his third-floor apartment, heard the commotion. He ran out of his apartment, down one flight of stairs, and leaped over the banister to the first floor, landing on her father's back and shoulders. Vincent continued the beat her father until he finally released her.

So it was, while her mother worked, her grandparents and four uncles reared Sylvia with love and care. Submersed in an environment rich with Sicilian dialect and Oklahoman her mother's accent, Sylvia grew up bilingual. What a combination!

One Sunday, when Sylvia was only five, the whole family packed up for an outing sponsored by the Sons of Italy at Wenham Lake in Wenham, Massachusetts. As the family was finishing their lunch that day, Vincent decided to go for a swim. When Vincent got up from the picnic table, his mother asked, "Where are you going?" Vincent replied, "I'm going swimming." His mother replied, "But you just finished eating." Vincent said, "Oh Ma," waved his hand as if to say goodbye, ran and dove into the water.

Sylvia, watched, him dive into the frigid lake water. At only five, she would have no perception of the events about to transpire. Vincent never came up from that dive. When he entered the cold, cold water, it was a shock to his system. It brought on a heart attack and he drowned.

Vincent was eighteen at the time. A handsome and popular young man, he was already a professional hairdresser for a large beauty salon, and had several women working under him. He entered the water at about 1:30 PM. For the rest of the afternoon, no one thought anything of the fact he wasn't seen. He was probably off talking to a girl or two.

By 5:00 PM, when the bus was being packed for the return trip home, the family began to wonder where Vincent was. After over an hour's search, it became apparent something was radically wrong. A rescue squad was called. They began dragging the lake, and soon, they found Vincent. When they pulled him from the water, he had grass in his fists as if he was trying to pull himself out. He had bloodsuckers attached, and small but noticeable holes about his face and body.

In those days, the dead were laid out not in a funeral home, but in the home of the deceased. In this case, he was laid out in his family's living room. The embalmer filled the small holes in his face with wax and applied makeup.

For three days, the family was present during the all-day-long visiting hours. It wasn't until 6:00 or 7:00 in the early evening that people simply stopped coming. Because Vincent was so popular, people came from all over the area. The news of the tragedy traveled like wildfire.

Sylvia, of course, was there as people came and went. No meals were served, however, and she would sit behind one of the living room chairs and be fed cookies to hold her to the next meal. Another odd thing also occurred several times during each day of the three-day viewing. Every so often, someone in the family would pick Sylvia up and have her kiss the corpse. She didn't seem to mind. He was, after all, one of her favorite uncles.

When they brought Vincent to the grave, Vincent's mother was inconsolable and totally out of control. Crying loudly, even screaming, she attempted to throw herself into the grave and onto the casket. Sylvia recalls this as a terrible scene.

Every so often, Sylvia's mother would take Sylvia to her mother's house for care to give her mother-in-law a rest. The scene there was totally different. Her maternal grandmother had five unmarried children at home, and the three youngest were all girls, Christina, was the youngest. In fact she was three months younger than Sylvia, born the following Christmas, Jenny was two years older than Sylvia, and Angelina four years older than Sylvia. Therefore, Sylvia had three females to play with.

When her mother took Sylvia to her mother's house, she would leave Sylvia there for a week. Her mother lived in Charlestown and she found it difficult to pack Sylvia up every morning and evening. Therefore, she would bring here there on the weekend and pick her up the following weekend.

One day, while Sylvia was staying in Charlestown, she was just looking out the window onto the street and she saw Jenny waiting on the sidewalk trying to cross

21

the street. Suddenly, she tried to run across the street and got hit by a car. She was badly hurt. However, by the grace of God, she did get well.

Another time, she and Christina decided to take a bubble bath. They succeeded in getting the tub loaded with bubbles, so well, that when they got in the tub, the bottom was very slippery and Sylvia slid under the water. Christina ran and got her mother to go to the bathroom. Miraculously, when the grandmother pulled Sylvia out, she was gasping for breath but was still alive. Her grandmother immediately called the doctor. Sylvia was bedridden all week. In those days, most of the working class did not own a phone. Therefore, her mother did not know what happened. When she arrived on the weekend, Sylvia was in bed. Her mother told her what had happened, and Sylvia was taken home. As a result, Sylvia grew up with a dread fear of water. She never did learn how to swim.

Then as if the loss of her uncle wasn't enough, her mother's father decided he wanted to move to San Jose, California. Sylvia now lost her maternal grandfather, grandmother, two uncles and three aunts. Sylvia missed them tremendously.

Another uncle, a great uncle (who was also named Vincent), lived just two blocks away. Sylvia would visit him and his family almost daily. Vincent was married and had one son and three daughters, two of whom were twins. One of the twins, Tina, would often baby sit for Sylvia. They were very close, and remained that way throughout their whole life. There was seven years difference between Tina and Sylvia.

When he was in his early fifties, Vincent was diagnosed with cancer. As it continued to worsen, he became very weak. He would walk around the apartment and ask Sylvia to walk with him, holding hands (as if a child of six would really be able to do anything if he fell). Perhaps he didn't fall for fear he might fall on top of her. He passed away in the summer of 1936.

So it was that Sylvia saw death at a very early age and it affected her deeply. With the loss of her Vincents, Sylvia became profoundly lonely.

Sylvia's mother was the second oldest child, but the first girl, she had an older brother. Because she was the oldest daughter, she was saddled with a lot of household chores and the actual bringing up of her siblings. Her mother was very resentful of this all of her life and definitely did not want a large family. Sylvia's father insisted, he wanted another child, a boy that he would call Vincent, and her mother finally conceded.

Because she was an only child, Sylvia would plead with her mother for a baby sister. At the age of six, Sylvia promised her mother that if she got a baby sister, she would do all her mother's food shopping to help out. Remember, Sylvia was only six years of age.

When she started going to school in the fall of 1936, this loneliness must have shown through. Miss McCloud, her first-grade teacher, would, from time to time, ask Sylvia to come to her, and she would pick her up and place her on her lap. Miss McCloud would continue teaching the class with Sylvia right there.

Years later, Sylvia was on the train. She met another of the school's teachers, Miss DeSantis, a best friend of her old teacher. Sylvia told her of the time spent on her teacher's lap. Miss DeSantis said, they both would do that whenever they felt a child needed special attention.

On September 19, 1936, when Sylvia was nearly seven, her sister Lydia was born. Her mother told her that since she wanted that baby so badly, every time she went out, she was to take Lydia with her. She did so, gladly. It was like she was playing house with a real live doll.

The family was living on the third floor of a three-story walkup, and the stairways and landings were so narrow, one could not store a baby carriage anywhere. Sylvia had to carry the baby everywhere. Her mother would bathe the baby, feed and clothe her (putting on a clean diaper, of course), before Sylvia took the baby out.

They went everywhere together, even to the theatre for a Saturday matinee. There was only one problem: Sylvia wasn't given any milk or change of diapers, so when the baby became in need of attention, she would have to take the baby home. From the day her sister was born until she was thirteen years old, Sylvia never saw a complete movie.

This went on for years, but by the time Sylvia was thirteen, Lydia was in school and had her own group of neighborhood friends. Sylvia implored her father to talk to Mom about the situation. Sylvia had her own friends and wanted to be released from her commitment. Her mother finally conceded the point, and Sylvia went on with her friends. Her mother felt she now was a family of three, Sylvia, Lydia, and her.

Sylvia's father was never faithful to his wife the entire marriage. There were always "extracurricular" activities. His attitude was that he had done her a favor by marrying her, and he would do as he pleased. At times, he was very open with his infidelity. Shortly after being wed, he was seeing a woman who lived near where he worked. He gave her a job bagging repaired shoes and keeping shoes in numerical order on the shelves. Sylvia's mother caught on. She took Sylvia to the shoe shop and confronted him, all to no avail.

Sylvia was never told of her birth being just a month after her parents were wed. Her parents covered this up by having occasions and playing with the dates. For instance, they threw a tenth-anniversary party when Sylvia was eight years old. It made everything seem correct.

But even then, her father was seeing yet another woman, and with all the gall in the world, invited her to this tenth-anniversary party. Sylvia wasn't dumb, and over the years had sneaking suspicions as to what was happening. It wasn't more than six months after the anniversary party that Sylvia's mother confided in her.

She told her she had gone to this other woman's home to talk with her, to tell her to leave her husband alone. The woman went to a closet and came out with a beautiful bathrobe., she showed her the price tag of $50.00. This was the year 1937, at that particular time the average pay, for the working class, was about $15.00

a week. She told Sylvia's mother it was a Christmas present from him. She was treated so well, she was not about to change the relationship.

This nearly caused a breakup of her parents. Her mother had thoughts of escaping, with her daughters, to California. She changed her mind, however, and stayed with him until the day he died. That affair lasted at least seven years, as far as Sylvia is aware.

One day, when she was thirteen, she decided to take a train to her father's shoe shop, which she did maybe once a week. He had hired a young boy to shine shoes. He lived with his parents over the shop and, since they both worked, they thought the boy's arrangement worked out fine. They were pleased and grateful that their son, Bill, not only had a job but someone to watch over him while they worked. This friendship between Sylvia's father and the boy's family lasted a lifetime.

On this particular day, when Sylvia arrived at the shop, her father didn't seem to be anywhere around. Only the shine boy, Bill, was there. When asked where her father was, Bill said he was down in the basement where he kept his leather supplies. Sylvia was told by her father never to go there because of rats. Bill, at this point, was calling loudly for her father, announcing that Sylvia was there.

When the father came up, he was with his girlfriend, and they quietly sneaked into a back room on the first floor. Not having heard them, Sylvia started walking to the back of the store and found her father and his girlfriend in casual conversation. It seems that the girl had brought some white flannel material that was to be cut up for shine cloths.

As the girlfriend was leaving, Sylvia joined her. They took the train together back to East Boston. During the trip, the girlfriend was trying to be nice. She really was anticipating marrying Sylvia's father, and thought that Sylvia and her sister Lydia would live with her. That pushed Sylvia over the edge. She told the woman if she were ever to be seen by Sylvia in her father's store again, she would throw her out bodily.

That was kind of funny: Sylvia, all of 102 pounds, handling a woman weighing well over 200. Such is what Sicilians are made of. She would have done it too.

Sylvia went directly to her aunt's house, the home of her father's younger brother. She was trembling and in tears from her anger. How dare that woman think she could replace her mother? Sylvia told her aunt all that had transpired, and asked that she tell her husband, and he, in turn, tell her grandfather. Her uncle did just as Sylvia requested. When her grandfather called her father on the carpet, he ordered him to break up with the other woman and, by the way, he was disinherited.

The breakup did occur, but her father, once again, hated Sylvia even more. He did not do anything to Sylvia at first, but he planned his revenge. He told her to be home every evening by nine o'clock. Sure enough, Sylvia landed home five minutes late one night, and her father was waiting for her.

There were four rooms in their apartment, all lined up in a row. Her beating started in the kitchen. Sylvia tried to retreat and escape the savage blows. When they finally were in the living room, there was nowhere left to go. He gave her yet another massive blow that knocked Sylvia on the floor on her back. He lifted his foot and gave a crushing stomp on her stomach. The blow took her breath away and she could not move.

Sylvia asked her mother to call a doctor, but her father intervened, He approached Sylvia saying, "Sylvia, we cannot call the doctor, if he sees you like this, they will put me in jail. knowing he would be arrested for abuse. After that attack, Sylvia's stomach continued to be a problem for many years. Her father must have had some feelings of guilt over the incident.

That Christmas, Sylvia's best friend, who she hadn't seen since the end of the summer, came to visit. Joan also came from a small family, and both of her parents worked. They were very particular about the way their children dressed. Joan may have been about twenty pounds heavier than she should have been but wore clothes that were custom tailored for her by a local designer. She always looked quite elegant, and that Christmas day was no exception.

Sylvia's father noted how nice Joan looked. When Joan left he said, "Why can't you dress like that?" Sylvia became furious and said to him, "You give Mom $25.00 a week to buy food, clothing, to pay the rent, and utilities, and you want me to look like that? Her mother has all her clothing custom made for her!"

With that, he took a $100.00 bill out of his wallet and told her to go buy herself an outfit. Having gone into Boston many times and done wishful-thinking window shopping, she now had the means. She took her mother to a very exclusive store and bought a very smart looking wool dress and a light blue fleece coat. Her father then took the family to a professional photographer with Sylvia in her new outfit. It was his way of showing the world what a wonderful father he was.

Chapter 2

Even through all of this stress and strain (or probably, because of it), Sylvia quickly grew into a dynamic and assertive young woman. In 1942, she was still only thirteen, but she knew that some sort of skill would be essential to be successful in a "man's world." Typing came to the forefront as a skill she could master.

At the age of thirteen, for thirty-five cents an hour, she got a job simply wrapping washcloths for eventual sale. It might not have been an exciting job, but she worked very hard and scuttled away every penny she could.

On the social scene, Sylvia was very outgoing and had a rather large group of friends. Neptune Road was the usual gathering place after dinner, and nearly every day, Sylvia would trek there to be with her friends. But there was one small problem: Sylvia's parents had dinner after her father closed down his shoe-repair shop. That put her arrival at Neptune Road a good hour after the others had congregated.

As she turned the corner of Bennington Street to Neptune Road, her friends would be waiting for her to approach. As soon as she did, all the girls would run for two blocks to meet her with their arms wide open, screaming her last name, "Caccamesi! Caccamesi!" They were happy to see her, and she was just as happy to see them. She only wished they wouldn't be so demonstrative.

Thirty-five cents an hour, part time, wasn't much. But eventually, she had enough money to buy a brand new, fifty-dollar portable Remington Remette typewriter. Every day after school, she worked with her new typewriter, honing her skills.

At fifteen, she interviewed for a part-time, after-school job in an insurance office, typing policies. She got it simply because of her typing skills. Later, she got a job with a roofing company. It was a small, two-girl office, and she typed correspondence of all sorts after school. Not only did she learn office work, but how offices worked. She would use this later to her advantage.

Also at the age of fifteen, Sylvia had her first boyfriend, Tony. They loved each other dearly. Most people agree there is something very special about a first love. This one was to be no exception. It was 1945, and World War II was winding down.

A strange thing happened one day. Tony came to visit every day after school. He was the type of person who, once he got in the habit of doing something, you could set your clock by it. So it was with these daily visits. At 3:00 PM every afternoon, Tony would be at her house.

For some reason, the boys on her street seemed to resent her having a boy-friend. Why, she didn't know. She didn't go out with any of them; she just played with them, and the girls, as anyone would in a community. One day, the boys got together and decided that they would gather in front of her house just at the time Tony was to arrive.

When Sylvia exited her house, she saw about six of the local boys sitting on the steps. Although courteous, she was getting rather uneasy as they chattered away about things unknown. She didn't want them there. To have Tony walk up and think she had been with various boyfriends would be too much to bear.

Suddenly, at his accustomed hour, almost out of the blue, it appeared as though Tony was looking at all of these boys in surprise. The look was so shocking, that all the boys quickly felt convicted of betrayal. Just as quickly, the figure turned around and ran away. Sylvia angrily dismissed the boys, and as they left, she ran after the phantom. Suddenly, the figure she followed seemed to vanish into thin air.

With nothing more left to do, she hurriedly began to walk the twelve blocks toward Tony's home, hoping she could see him and explain. When she was two blocks from his house, she saw Tony walking in her direction. When asked why he had run away, Tony, with a puzzled look on his face, told Sylvia that he had just left his house.

Equally puzzled, this was the strangest thing Sylvia had yet encountered. Honestly, she still thinks it was an angel sent to protect her by frightening the boys so they would leave and not be there when Tony arrived. Also, coincidently, was the fact that Tony was late arriving, as though he had been detained in order for the road to be clear.

Tony was always a gentleman with Sylvia. Frequently, they would go to dances sponsored by the city of Boston. These dances were held in the local school's play-ground every Saturday night. It was the Big Band era. Sylvia loved to dance up a storm. Tony did not, or should we say, could not. Because in later years, he told Sylvia that, as a boy he wished he could dance like Fred Astaire.

Sylvia didn't know this, or she would have gladly taught him how to dance. As one of the most handsome boys, he'd would instead, circulate among the girls while Sylvia danced, but always insisted on escorting Sylvia home at the end of the dance.

One night, Tony let Sylvia know that he was going to leave the dance to take home Cookie, a local girl. He instructed Sylvia to wait for his return, and told a friend to stay with her. When he returned, he told Sylvia that Cookie had asked him to go steady. He turned her down, stating, "I don't love you. I love Sylvia."

The following Saturday, Sylvia was at local movie theater, when a friend came in and told her that Cookie was in the lobby with about fifty girls who were intending to beat her up. Sylvia didn't know what to make of this. During the intermission, she walked down to the lobby to see what was going on.

Sure enough, they were all there. She confronted Cookie, asking if she was looking for her. Cookie told her she was upset because Tony had told her he loved Sylvia and not her. The Sicilian in Sylvia came to the front. She got in Cookie's face and told her that if she couldn't get the man she wanted, she shouldn't blame her. All the girls heard this, thought about it for a short time, agreed with Sylvia, and left.

One day, Tony arrived at Sylvia's house, and happily announced, that his three older brothers had come home from the war. Two were in the navy and one was in the army, and all were well, this was the summer of 1945. When Tony went back home, he proudly announced he had a girlfriend. The brothers quickly tried to discourage him. They told him he was too young to be tied down, and that he should be free to go with whomever he wished. The more they talked to him, the better the idea sounded.

Tony had just turned sixteen years of age on May 29, and at sixteen years of age, decided to take his brothers' advice. Tony went to Sylvia's home to announce that he no longer wanted to go steady. For three months, she was terribly broken-hearted and could not eat. At the age of fifteen, the loss of her love was devastating.

A strange thing happened, during those three months. Tony would still visit her from time to time as though nothing happened. During this period Sylvia received her graduation picture for the year 1947, a year in advance. The next time he came to visit, she showed him the picture that was going to appear in the year book.

He asked her if he could borrow it for a while, he said he wanted to show his brothers his girlfriend. He still referred to Sylvia as his girlfriend. She consented, but told him that was the only picture she had and wanted it back.

Tony took the picture home and proudly showed it to the whole family. His sister Marie was very curious and wanted some how to meet Sylvia. One day, Marie was walking down her street and saw Sylvia, she recognized her by the picture. She told her friend that she thought that girl was Tony's girlfriend.

Her friend told her that Sylvia came there often. She knew Patricia, who went to the same school she did. She also told her, that Sylvia and Patricia went to the local girls' club every Wednesday night to dance. No boys were allowed there. They simply danced to records for their own enjoyment. Marie told her friend she would like to go to the club the following Wednesday.

That Wednesday, Sylvia and Patricia went to the dance as usual. While they were dancing, Marie and her friend came in. She walked over to Sylvia, cut into the dance, picked Sylvia up with both arms and swung her all around. Sylvia was surprised to say the least, in her mind she thought, "Who is this?" When she looked closely, Marie's resemblance to Tony was unmistakable. Needless to say, they became very good friends.

Chapter 3

It was a short while later that a neighbor, Jane, suggested that she become a part of her new group of friends. Coincidently, Tony was also a member. Jane told Sylvia that Tony had suggested that she invite Sylvia to become a part of this group. Even given the breakup with Tony, she agreed.

Sometime later, a young man who lived in the area approached Sylvia. Tony sensed right away what this young man was up to, and quickly came close by. She introduced him to Tony, and after the introduction, the young man, with Tony right there, asked her for a date to the movie theater the following evening.

Evidently, Tony didn't care for the idea and instructed all his male friends to go to the Seville Theatre the next night and report to him all that went on. It turned out there was absolutely nothing to report.

Tony always considered Sylvia to be untouchable. He always treated her with great respect and politeness. He liked having Sylvia as a friend. Through the years, this relationship would prove to be on-again, off-again. To this day, Sylvia admits that Tony was the true love of her life. The problem was, Tony would continue to test their relationship.

The day after her date, when she arrived on Chelsea Street for the usual gathering, Tony approached her and asked, "Did you have a nice time at the movies last night?" Sylvia was going to have none of this, and taking Tony's arm, led him away from the group. She said, "Let's take a walk." As they began their walk, the whole group of twelve girls and boys formed a double line behind them and followed them. It looked like a mini procession.

She took the lead, pointing out that it was he who wanted to break up, not she. He tried to qualify the breakup by pointing out it was not that he didn't love her. It was simply that they were too young. Sylvia didn't buy this distinction, but agreed to a mutual-admiration-society type of relationship. Either could date whomever. It was stipulated that when they were older, say about twenty or twenty-one, they would get back together and get married.

"Till the End of Time" a record breaking song, sung by the very popular singer Perry Como became their love song. The melody was taken from Chopin's

Polonaise No.6. At the time, that Tony proposed the idea, it sounded like a good idea, but unfortunately, it didn't work out.

Tony did exactly what they had agreed to. After all, it was his idea, being very honest as always, he would take girls out right under Sylvia's nose. She, however, didn't go out with anyone for months, she was so hurt. When she saw him going on a date, the hurt only increased.

The next time Tony's sister saw Sylvia, she asked her if she could have the picture, Tony had shown the family. Sylvia agreed. To this day, Sylvia believes Tony put her up to it. One day Marie suggested to all her friends that they should all go dancing at the Oceanview Ballroom on Revere Beach.

This also included Sylvia who was now a part of Marie's group of friends. She suggested that Sylvia meet her at her house the following Saturday, and then they would meet the rest of the group and all leave together. Sylvia always looked much older than her age, she could easily pass for twenty.

Sylvia got all dressed up to go dancing and went to Marie's house. She thought all that was going to happen was that she would ring the bell and Marie would come out. However, Marie had other plans. She had orchestrated this scenario so that the whole family could meet Sylvia. When Sylvia rang the bell, Marie invited her in and directed her to the kitchen.

There in a semi-circle, in the kitchen were all four of Tony's brothers. They must have envisioned a very immature looking young girl. After all they had only seen her face in a portrait. The look on their faces was almost one of shock. They just gaped at her. Sylvia felt very uncomfortable. Tony, however, was grinning from ear to ear. Sylvia was glad to get out of there. From then on, Sylvia went over to the house to visit Marie often.

One day Sylvia's cousin Tina went to visit Sylvia. She had been going steady since her high school days, but unfortunately, WWII broke out and soon after her boyfriend Joe graduated high school he had to go into the service. Tina and Joe kept in touch with each other through letters and Joe, too, had returned home and Joe and Tina were engaged.

Tina came to tell Sylvia the good news and asked her if she would be a bridesmaid at her wedding. Sylvia was thrilled. She was still only fifteen years of age, but looked much older. When the wedding date was set and the invitations were printed, Sylvia asked Tina if she could have two invitations to invite Tony's brothers. She was very accommodating and two of Tony's older brothers came to the wedding.

Tina's wedding gown was beautiful. It was made by a wedding gown designer who lived on the second floor of the home of Joe's parents. She had been a professional designer in Italy before coming to America.

It was October 5, 1945: Sylvia's sixteenth birthday party. She invited all of her friends from Chelsea Street, including Tony. He gave her a present that was very meaningful, a gold-plated cross. Tony didn't have much money, so it was quite a financial stretch for him. Sylvia kept the cross and treasured it well into her fifties—when she lost it.

The following Christmas, Sylvia invited the same group of friends to her house. Knowing her parents celebrated Christmas at her paternal grandparents' home, Sylvia had a private Christmas party at her own home. She kept this party a secret from her parents.

At one point, Tony took Sylvia away from her friends into a private room. He kissed her so very passionately several times and then almost in a heart breaking voice, blurted out, "Syl, I love you." Sylvia never forgot that very precious moment and his profession of love.

Then the inevitable happened. The following spring, a local young man came home from the navy. He saw Sylvia at Woolworth's five-and-ten-cent Store and asked her for a date. Having known Ted since about thirteen, she accepted. Ted immediately became very serious about a relationship with Sylvia, and would even visit her mother while Sylvia was at work.

At one point, he asked her mother if Sylvia would accept an engagement ring. Her mother knew that she still cared for Tony, and told Ted she didn't think it was a good idea. But Ted persisted. He asked Sylvia if he could see her on a Sunday evening. This was unusual, because they were only seeing each other on Saturday evenings. They would go dancing, and Sylvia loved it.

To have a Sunday date and go to the movies was going to escalate their dating time. Worse, he also mentioned that he would like to go steady! Since the relationship with Tony was on the outs, she agreed to think about it for a week. Then, she would give him an answer about the going steady thing.

It was quite obvious the issues with Tony were resentful and hurtful. Knowing that she was bound to see Tony during that week, depending on what transpired, she would know what her answer to Ted would be. Even though she made the agreement with Tony, she was very disheartened. She was still a sixteen-year-old child, and didn't have the patience she now feels she should have had.

Tony did go to visit her. He said it seemed to him that they were not seeing enough of one another, and it seemed as though they were drifting further and further apart. She made a date with Tony for the following Sunday afternoon. She now had a date with Tony in the afternoon and with Ted that same evening. The date with Tony would determine her future.

That Sunday afternoon, she waited patiently for Tony to arrive. The longer she waited, the more hurt she felt. She eventually came to the realization that he was not going to show.

That evening, Ted arrived early. He was anxiously awaiting her answer. She was so upset with Tony that when Ted asked her if she had arrived at a decision, she quickly said that she would go steady with him. Now she had to tell Tony of her decision.

The following day, Sylvia went to Tony's house to talk to him. She informed him that she was now going steady with someone else. Tony was obviously very hurt. When Sylvia asked, "Why didn't you come to my house as planned, Sunday afternoon?" He said, "I ran into one of your neighbors, who told me you were going steady. Therefore, I couldn't see any point in keeping the Sunday afternoon date." Sylvia could not understand why he would believe such a thing without even talking to her first. Dejected, Sylvia simply left.

Later, Sylvia was with Tony's sister Marie. Marie told Sylvia that at age seventeen Tony had his parents sign a consent form so that he could join the army. When he began packing to leave, he went into his drawer where he kept Sylvia's portrait.

When Marie asked Sylvia if she could have the portrait, she took it out of Tony's drawer and put it in her drawer. Tony was unaware of the switch. When he couldn't find the portrait, he began yelling at his sister, "Where's Sylvia's picture? Where's Sylvia's picture?" She took it out of her drawer, and said "Here, take it."

He packed it with the rest of his belongings and took it with him. She recounted this story to Sylvia, in the hope that she would realize how much he really loved her. But, at this point the damage had been done, and Sylvia could not possibly see any way of turning back.

Sylvia was saddened by the way things worked out she always expected that they would be seeing each other when her senior prom was due, but this was not to be. The designer that made Tina's wedding gown made Sylvia's prom gown. It was a beautiful light blue gown with silver stars and quarter moons all over the bottom half of the dress and Ted was her escort.

Chapter 4

After a few months of Sylvia going steady with Ted, Sylvia's father hired him to work in the shoe shop. Ted had told him of a government training program through which a company could get half an employee's pay subsidized by the government. Ted became an apprentice. Of his $50.00 per week salary, the boss had to pay only $25.00. This was just a way for her father to get cheap labor.

Ted saw it as a way to get trained and possibly take over the business or at least get financial help later to start his own business. The financial help, he thought, would of course come from Sylvia's father. Ted thought it was his duty! Again, each one was looking out for himself.

Sylvia and Ted were now making plans to be married. Since this was right after World War II and a majority of the servicemen were home, finding a place to rent was virtually impossible. The GI Bill, however, allowed veterans to buy a house with no money down.

That was now the plan. They opened up a joint bank account and began saving for furnishings and wedding costs. It turned out that during their year-and-a-half courtship, they gathered enough money to not only pay cash for her gown and his tux, but for furnishings, silverware, nearly everything they needed for their new life together.

In 1947, six months into the courtship, Ted purchased a three-family walk-up in Dorchester, Massachusetts. It was in an Irish community that, at the time, was a fairly poor one. But the rent from the first and third-floor apartments—a hefty $25.00 each—paid for the mortgage.

The second floor, which was to be Sylvia and Ted's home, needed a lot of cosmetic work. For the next year, by working evenings and weekends, doing a little at a time, the two flights of stairs were painted and layers and layers of wallpaper were removed and tons of clean-up was performed. An awful lot of work was done and completed by the time they were married.

Ted was always a gentleman during this time. She thought she knew him fairly well. However, he tried to put Sylvia in an emotional closet, refusing to let her have any friends, even denying her the simple pleasure of saying hello to someone on the street. Sylvia knew he was being overly demanding, but somehow felt he just cared for her and wanted her complete attention. This should have raised a red flag of warning, but even if it had, she would have ignored it.

While Sylvia was making plans for an after-high-school-graduation wedding, she was receiving pictures of Tony in his army uniform. She wrote back and told him she was very sorry, but she could not continue answering his letters, it would be fruitless since she was getting married.

Sylvia later found out that Ted's parents were both alcoholics. His father's first wife was quite beautiful. Over a period of years, he became convinced that she was having an affair. In an argument that ensued, he picked his wife up and sat her on a hot cast iron stove that led to a divorce.

His second wife was not attractive, and when Ted's father began courting her, she had never had anyone before take an interest in her, she quickly latched onto him. His father's drinking continued, and she simply joined in. This pattern of behavior was passed along to Ted.

A year and a half after she began going with Ted, they made plans for their wedding. The wedding gown was made by the same designer that made Tina's wedding gown and she made all of the gowns for six bridesmaids. They were all duplicates of her prom gown except the stars and moons were left out and they were in various pastel shades, it was a rainbow wedding. She also had a flower girl and ring bearer. The flower girls gown was also made by the same designer, it was a replica of the bride's gown in miniature, she was a miniature bride. Even the wedding rings were very much like Tina's. Sylvia idolized her cousin Tina.

Bride Sylvia with a young cousin

Sylvia and Ted were married on April 4, 1948, ten months after she graduated high school. The courtship was a very nice one, and Ted seemed very caring.

However, the day after the wedding, Ted's demeanor did a one hundred and eighty degree turn, His attitude changed completely. To him, Sylvia had become a piece of property the very night of their wedding.

Sylvia rationalized he was perhaps stressed out because of all the excitement of the wedding day. A week passed, but his attitude did not change. Sylvia confronted him asking, "Ted, why are you acting this way?" His reply was, "Now you are married to me, now you are stuck to me." He was bossy, rude, and greedy. He was always expecting others, especially Sylvia, to do for him.

It was a rude awakening for her. The year-and-a-half courtship was nothing but one big act by Ted. This realization, however, did nothing for Sylvia. Her grandmother taught her that a woman should be married to only one man. So, for better or worse, Sylvia carried on.

She became pregnant within a matter of weeks of her marriage. This first pregnancy, however, did not go well. She was terribly sick, so much so that when she was three months along, she just had to go to the hospital. She stopped by her father's shop to tell her husband and father that she was headed for the hospital, but neither Ted nor her father offered to take her.

In July of 1948, she was admitted with a blood pressure of thirty over forty and suffering from severe dehydration due to constant vomiting. She couldn't hold anything down for the best of three months. The hospital staff was so concerned about her prognosis they sent a priest to her to give her last rites.

When the priest walked into her room, she became very frightened. He told her he came to hear her confession. Startled even more, Sylvia asked, "Why Father, do I need it?" He looked and Sylvia and replied, "Let's wait and see," and left. God was good and pulled her through, another example of God's miraculous intervention.

Her husband was totally uncaring through all this. As a matter of fact, he would complain that he'd wake up every morning to Sylvia's nausea. If she didn't do something that needed doing, his snide remarks cut deeply. All he cared about was Ted.

Their first Christmas Eve was the worse she had ever experienced. Here she was, pregnant with her first child, due on January 16, 1949, and was waiting for her husband to come home so that they could spend some time together. She waited and waited and waited. When he finally arrived home, he was so drunk he and could barely stand up. Staggering, he made his way to the kitchen, turned to face her, and greeted Sylvia with a loud "Merry Christmas" before he passed out in front of her.

She tried picking him up and taking him to bed, but he was like dead weight. Little by little, she dragged him into the bedroom and finally managed to get him in bed. Throughout the night, each time he would roll over and face her, he would call her name—and vomit. This happened four times in the course of the night, and each time, Sylvia had to change the linen on the bed and wash up. By morning, she was exhausted. To say the least, she was a very unhappy woman.

Nine months and twelve days after she was married, her daughter Lynda Marie was born. Fourteen months later, March 22, 1950, her second child, Teddie Junior, was born. Her pregnancy had progressed with few problems, but the baby had the problems this time. He was born three weeks early. His lungs hadn't expanded and he had yellow jaundice. After he was hospitalized for a month, the doctors sent him home to die. Once again God was good: Teddie Junior survived.

Still, her husband continued to show no sign of caring about anyone or anything. He would come home after work and do nothing but complain that he was tired. He would eat his supper, watch TV, drink a half-gallon bottle of beer, and then go to bed.

Chapter 5

After the close of the war, the army was sending Tony to Germany on regular trips by ship. He was sent to pick up patients who had mental breakdowns and return them to the States. He would leave from Brooklyn, New York only to re-enter the terrible post-war conditions in Germany many times. He took on the role of a male nurse. Unfortunately, in part because of the deplorable conditions in Germany, Tony contacted tuberculosis. As was frequently done back then, his family was very secretive about his illness.

Wherever Sylvia went, she would seem to run into people who knew Tony. They would tell her they heard Tony was in the hospital. Everyone who knew him was wondering what was wrong. One of his father's friends, a man in his sixties, asked his father what was wrong with Tony.

The father did not want to tell him the truth, because tuberculosis was a terribly dreaded illness once called consumption. Therefore, he fabricated the story that he had a venereal disease. This seemed much more macho to him. Ironically, that was Patricia's father.

One day, Sylvia went to visit Patricia and she told Sylvia, Tony had a venereal disease. The word spread like wild fire. Sylvia could not believe that story. She could not believe Tony would be so stupid as to allow himself to contact a venereal disease. Sylvia went to visit Tony's sister, Marie and asked her what was wrong with Tony. She told her that he had tuberculosis and was being hospitalized at a veteran's tuberculosis hospital in Rutland, Massachusetts

At that time, the hospital staff was uncertain what they could do. Both of his lungs were infected. Therefore, removing one lung was not an option. Two years earlier, penicillin and streptomycin had become the treatment of choice, in hopes it might eradicate the disease. As in all cases, only time would tell. Finally after two and a half years, 1n 1952, Tony was sent home. Tony's Sister told Sylvia when he came home.

Sylvia decided that she would call and wish him well. Sylvia did not know who would answer the phone. She was very surprised when he answered. When he returned home, he had arranged to have a phone installed in his bedroom, on a night stand right next to his bed.

She recognized his voice immediately, even though it was the first time that she ever heard it over a telephone. They had always talked face to face. He was a boy then, and a man now, yet she knew it was him. Before he could say another word, Sylvia said, "I'm glad that you are well and back home. Immediately Tony recognized her voice, asking, "Is that you?"

Just as she had recognized him from his simple, "Hello?" For some unknown reason, he asked a favor: He asked her to call back in a week. He never mentioned her name. Sylvia didn't know why he wanted her to call back in a week, but she never questioned his request.

The following weekend, Ted made arrangements, once again, for Sylvia and Ted to visit his sister. This time, the scenario took a very different twist. Ted's brother-in-law approached with a proposition. He told her that Ted, Ted's sister and her husband had a meeting and agreed to a wife swapping deal. Ted with his sister, and if Sylvia agreed, she would be the brother-in-law's playmate. Sylvia was shocked hurt and furious.

Now she knew why Ted always put his sister before her, and why they had to go to visit them every weekend. She also realized this incest must have been going on for years. How could she possibly compete with this relationship between brother and sister?

Now her Sicilian temper flew. To think that her own husband would willingly turn her over to another man was more than she could bear. She looked Jack straight in the eye and said, "Let me tell you something, no man will ever touch me that I don't want." End of discussion. From then on, Sylvia lost all respect for her husband, she could barely stand to look at him straight in the eye.

The following day marked a week since she spoke to Tony, she called him as promised. When he answered the phone, he immediately told her that within that week, he had gone to get his driver's license and had purchased a brand new 1952 Pontiac Chieftain.

Since he had been in the hospital for two and a half years and collecting his disability pension for that amount of time, he could well afford it. He then asked for Sylvia's address and directions how to get to there. He wanted to talk to her face to face. Sylvia complied, and within an hour, he was knocking at her door.

He looked very handsome and was well-dressed. They met for about an hour and, within that time, Tony asked if there was some way that they could arrange to meet on occasion. Knowing she was entering dangerous territory, Sylvia agreed.

They chatted a while more, and then Tony pleaded with Sylvia, "Syl, please." Sylvia conceded. Each Saturday, she hired a babysitter so that she could go to East Boston and purchase meat for the week. She was very particular about the quality of the food she and her family ate, and didn't care for the quality of meat sold locally.

Seeing that as an opportunity, the plan was made. They would meet for a few hours after the shopping trips, but Sylvia had to be home to cook dinner. This situation soon escalated when Sylvia started to work evenings. She told her husband that the job required seven nights a week. In reality, she was working six nights so that she could spend one evening a week with Tony.

This went on for nearly two years. During that time, Tony taught Sylvia how to drive a car. Every so often he would let her do the driving. They went on long drives to the beautiful shores of Rockport. It was 1952, at that time, Rockport was a quiet little town. When they went on the Beach on Saturdays there were only a few people on the beach. It got so the residents got to know Sylvia and Tony and say hello.

At lunch Tony and Sylvia would go to a local takeout restaurant that featured the meat of one whole lobster in a bun, cost ninety nine cents. As the years went on, there was a TV series that was filmed in Rockport. At the end of each episode, there was a caption that stated all the scenes were filmed in Rockport.

From then on people came to Rockport in droves. Sometimes they would go to Breakheart Reservation in Saugus, where they had cook outs. These weekly retreats with Tony were for Sylvia, her escape from a very bad situation at home that she looked forward to.

Was it Ted's deriding possessiveness, Sylvia's utter contempt for Ted, or her love for Tony that drove her? Only time would tell. Then the inevitable happened: Tony's tuberculosis reared its ugly head again. Tony knew he had to go back to the hospital, and the next time he saw Sylvia, he told her. Sylvia was devastated.

Tony didn't know what to do with his car. He feared if the car stayed at his house, doing nothing, for a long period of time, it would rot away. He asked Sylvia if she would like to use it. Sylvia had to refuse him. How could she ever explain where she got the new car. He finally gave it to another member of the family to use.

Back to the VA Hospital he went, this time for one year. She was very concerned and missed him terribly. She thought of all of the stories he told her of his efforts to make the best of his first two-and-a-half-year stay.

He had taken classes in mathematics, right up through calculus. His teacher was amazed how as he grew, he became able to do problems in his head. He was taught to make necklaces and bracelets out of silver, truly nice pieces. He learned to type, but gave it up. It was 1951 and he thought it was a bit too much of a "girl thing."

There was a piano in the hospital basement, and when he felt well enough, he found it and taught himself to play. He had wanted to be a composer in his early years and felt that was a primary motivating factor now. He became so good, in fact, that a priest, hearing the piano, followed the music to Tony and complimented him on his skill, stating, "You have a wonderful touch."

Tony never told his family about his new talent, however. He knew his father would not have approved. When he was young, his father once asked Tony what he would like to be. He told of his desire to be a composer. His father replied sarcastically, "When you grow up, you will sing another tune." With that Tony dropped the subject and never mentioned it again.

How ironic it would be, because Tony loved music. For a boy who grew up in the tough East Boston neighborhood, playing the piano would have been too much of a "sissy" thing. So he kept his skill and love for music to himself for the most part. But, of course, Sylvia was the only other person, outside of the people in the hospital, who knew. He would share all of his private loves and thoughts with her.

Tony loved all types of music, from Chopin and Tchaikovsky to the Big Band sounds, Stan Kenton's progressive jazz, and everything in between. Most of all, he loved, love songs. Sylvia adored love songs, too. As mentioned earlier the music adapted from Chopin's Polonaise No. 6, Perry Como's "Till the End of Time" became Tony and Sylvia's love song. One of the patients once called him an incurable romantic.

When Sylvia finally worked up the courage to visit Tony in the hospital, he told her, among other things, that he had told the other patients close to him about her. In a four-bed ward, the others would vacate the room when Sylvia came to visit, so she and Tony could be alone. One patient, on his way out, remarked to Tony that they were such a perfect couple they even looked alike.

When Tony went back to the hospital that second time, Sylvia avoided her husband as much as she possibly could. Eventually, he would no longer take no for an answer, and three months after Tony entered the hospital, Sylvia became pregnant with her third child.

She had gone to see Tony at the hospital only once before she found out she was pregnant. After that, she sent him a letter saying they should halt this relationship; after all, she was a married woman. She did not dare tell him she was pregnant.

Chapter 6

Nine months later, on August 30, 1954, her son Dan was born during a full-blown hurricane named Carol. After the delivery, they took Sylvia back to her ward and her bed that was directly under a huge picture window. The fierce winds blew in the room's window, and tiny shards of broken glass fell all over her bed. Fortunately, the glass blew over her head and the pieces landed on the sheets covering her. The nurses quickly rolled up all the glass in the sheets and moved Sylvia into a semi-private room.

After the delivery of the other two children, she had felt like a new woman. Now she was in terrible pain and could hardly move. Sylvia sensed something was wrong, and asked a nurse to send for her doctor. After he examined her, he simply ordered some warm baths and claimed nothing was wrong. In reality, the problem was that he had not removed all of the afterbirth.

The hospital discharged her and sent her home with the baby, but things got increasingly worse. Now she was caring for three small children while bent at the waist; she could not straighten. After a week in this condition, she called her private doctor. Yet another hurricane, Edna, was blowing during that house call. The doctor examined her and told her to re-admit herself to the hospital she had come from. He told her she had peritonitis, an inflammation of the wall of her abdomen covering the organs within. He did not want to treat her, because he was not responsible for the damage done.

As the doctor returned to his office, he dropped in to see Sylvia's father at the shoe shop. Her father scolded the doctor about being out in such weather. The doctor replied, "I was out taking care of your daughter." He explained what his diagnosis was and told him to take Sylvia to the hospital quickly or she would die.

Very concerned, her father left the shop immediately, he went to her house, and took Sylvia back to the hospital. There were trees falling everywhere. With her condition now known, the hospital could no longer deny the damage that had been done.

As if to appease the situation, she was placed in the most expensive section of the institution. One doctor was overheard telling others to follow Sylvia's case closely, because they might not ever see another case like it. They honestly did not know what to do for her. She lay on her bed with a high fever and could not even move from side to side because the pain was so bad.

She was worried about her children, but could do nothing. She implored God for help, praying that if He really wanted to take her, He was going to have to see that her children were taken care of. As she requested, it came to be that Ted's younger sister, Ida, with one little girl of her own, would go over to Sylvia's house and care for her children while she was in the hospital.

Right after she turned her fate over to God, the doctors began experimenting with a combination of penicillin and streptomycin, which was also Tony's miracle drug. That miraculously began to clear up the infection. After about two weeks of this treatment, Sylvia was well enough to return home. Once again, God gave the cure to the doctors and pulled her through. Walking slowly and still a bit bent over, she somehow managed to care for her children.

Tony and Sylvia were released from their hospitals at about the same time. As soon as Tony got home, every Saturday afternoon, he would take his car and travel the route he knew Sylvia would take at the exact time she should have been there in search of her. It took Sylvia approximately one month before she even tried to take the trip on Saturday. When she did go to do her meat shopping, Tony found her, walking very slowly and still bent over. He pulled to the curb and told her to get in the car. He asked what had happened to her and she explained the long ordeal. They resumed their Saturday routine as if nothing at all had happened in the intervening years. Later, Tony even made her a silver necklace and bracelet that she treasured for years.

While living in Dorchester for seven years, Sylvia noticed the gradual deterioration of the neighborhood. Just because she and Ted were not getting along did not stop her from wanting a better life for her children, and a better location in which to raise them.

It was now the winter of 1954. She started searching for a single-family house in the city of Revere, where her sister lived. After a few weeks of searching, she found a small, ten-year-old cape-style house she thought would be just right, and that she could afford.

Because they had spent only $5,000.00 on their first home, they could still afford to buy another on the GI Bill. The Cape was priced at a whopping $10,200.00, and required a $200.00 down payment. Sylvia arranged for the purchase of the property without Ted ever going to see it. When he finally did, he approved of the house and the move. What he did not know, however, was that Sylvia had already made the down payment. The mortgage payment was a nearly exorbitant $100.00 every single month.

Problems, however, continued to escalate with Ted. One evening, as Sylvia exited her home to go to work, she noticed a neighborhood girl talking with some boys in a car just outside her house. The girl was all of fifteen, and cajoled the boys to take Sylvia to the train station instead of using a cab. She thought she was doing Sylvia a favor, and although she was, Ted noticed, and began accusing her of going out on a date with the young boys. His viciousness came out again. He began beating her.

In hopes of getting away, she ran toward their bathroom with Ted in close pursuit. She didn't make it. He caught her just past the door and struck such a blow that she fell over the tub, grabbing a towel rack to keep from hitting the hard porcelain. The towel bar didn't hold, however, and ripped from the wall. Now armed, she faced him. Ted backed off and pleaded, "Don't hit me, don't hit me." Some husband! He had given Sylvia a bloody cut over her eye. She simply ignored him and left.

The tryst with Tony continued that very night after the beating. On a double date with Tony's friend and girlfriend, sitting in the back seat, Tony could not help but notice the cut over her eye. She quietly told him that Ted was responsible.

The next day, she called the police. The cut and bruises were clearly visible as they talked with her. They decided to wait until Ted came from work, and then they would arrest and book him. That is exactly what happened. Ted called his father and got bailed out. It was the very next day that they appeared in court. After all was said and done, Ted received only a scolding from the judge.

During the hearing, as she was telling her story, he asked her how many times she had been beaten during their marriage of nine years. Sylvia briefly outlined the various times. The judge then asked if any of her children had ever been in his or any other court.

At first, she didn't understand the question, so the judge rephrased it slightly, asking if any of her children had been in his courtroom, charged with any crime. Shocked, Sylvia adamantly responded that they had not. The judge chided Sylvia, insisting that if her children were to continue witnessing this abuse, he guaranteed her that he would see them in his court, and that she was not doing her children any favor by staying in this abusive relationship.

This drove Sylvia to want to get her driver's license, and purchase a 1956 Ford Customline. She had the down payment and paid the rest monthly with the wages she received.

Not long after, on a Sunday afternoon, Ted began an argument over nothing. She didn't understand what brought this on. At one point, Ted even suggested, with many expletives, that she just leave. His words, more than ever before, cut into her like knives. Sylvia, lost it completely. Knowing the words but having never sworn before, she let loose. Every time he would open his mouth to continue his tirade, Sylvia shut him up with, her own expletives – over and over and over again. Poor Ted was shocked.

Sylvia took her children and went to her parents' home. After about a three-hour cooling down period, she returned home to find Ted had packed up his things and was gone. Sylvia stayed home from work the following day, and changed all of the locks in the house. However, she had not thought to change the locks on her car. Several mornings later, as she was leaving the house for work, she saw that there was no car in the driveway. She knew Ted was living with his sister, so, on a covert mission at 5:00 A. M., she hired a cab and got the car back. Revenge was indeed a dish best served cold.

At that time, Ted was seeing a seventeen-year-old girl and was blaming Sylvia for his infidelity. His family was well aware of what was going on, and his mother even had a picture of the girl on her bureau.

Sylvia heard later that although he wanted to marry his seventeen-year-old girl-friend, the girl's father had found out about the tryst with the thirty-one-year-old Ted, about his marriage, and about his children, and made sure that the relationship ended.

Chapter 7

Ted and Sylvia were separated for about a year when Tony again had to re-enter the hospital for another bout with tuberculosis.

Sylvia was now working full time as secretary to the president of a company that manufactured gift-wrapping paper and ribbon. Each day after work, she would pack her children into her car and drive out to the Rutland, MA, hospital, which was a one-hour ride. She would visit with Tony for about an hour and return home. On Saturday, she would hire a babysitter and visit him (without taking her children) so that she could spend three to four hours with him. As he was getting a little better, from time to time, the hospital would allow him to go home on weekends.

The Mondays after those weekends, she would take him back to the hospital. Those times were extremely hard on Tony. Once he was out of the hospital, he did not want to go back. But he did. Sylvia could feel his anxiety grow as they got closer and closer to the hospital. This went on for nearly two months. Something had to give.

On a Saturday afternoon in June of 1959, as she was approaching the driveway of the hospital, she heard Tony calling out. He wanted her to park in an area close to a door of the hospital. Soon, Tony approached the car, fully dressed. He got into the car and told her to drive. He had decided to leave the hospital without permission and never return. Sylvia was a bit apprehensive. She did as requested. She drove out of the hospital grounds and passed the guards with no problem. She was quite concerned; she didn't know what was going to happen next.

Tony instructed her to drive to his home in East Boston. When they arrived in the city, he asked Sylvia to stop near a phone booth. He called his brother and instructed him to go to the bank and take out the money that he had accumulated. His brother did exactly as requested. Tony told her that he wanted her to do three things for him: start divorce proceedings, quit her job, and take care of him. He told her he would take care of the expenses. Expenses be hanged, Sylvia's love for Tony and no such for Ted, she could do nothing but help him.

They then drove out to Salisbury, where he rented a motel room. That day, Sylvia purchased their dinner and they ate in the motel room. At this point, Sylvia's daughter was twelve years old and capable of caring for her younger brothers for a few hours at a time. Sylvia would leave her daughter some money in case they needed anything. She did return home, however, leaving Tony in the motel, so she could check on her children. It was June and the children were out of school.

The following Monday morning, Sylvia called work, as Tony requested, and told the receptionist to tell her boss that she would no longer be working there. Her mother later told her that her boss was very upset. He had called her house to try to find out why Sylvia quit. Her mother didn't know, but assumed that the pay was not enough and that was what she told him. He asked, "If she needed more money, why didn't she ask me?" Her mother just said she didn't know. She suggested that Sylvia call him. When she had a chance, she called the office and the manager answered. Sylvia asked for the president, but was told that he was not there. He had a heart attack and was very ill at home. She gave Sylvia his home phone and she called his house. His wife answered the phone and told Sylvia that he was very ill and did not allow her to speak to him. Later, Sylvia found out he passed away.

One day, while she was rummaging through her pocketbook, Sylvia found a letter that had been given to her by a former co-worker. It contained a prayer for physical healing. She had been carrying this prayer around for a few years, as though she felt that sooner or later she might need it. Now, here she was, with an ill Tony, in a motel room. As Tony slept, she took out the letter, laid her hand on his body, and prayed the prayer.

Each day, Sylvia would feed Tony breakfast, then travel the forty miles home to look after her children. Returning to Tony for an early lunch, they would eat and talk. She then would return home to give her children lunch. The same thing happened for dinner. This continued for about a month. She would notice a slight improvement in Tony's condition each day. Soon, they began to realize they would have to find a less expensive place to live. Tony's money was beginning to dwindle.

In July of 1959, they moved to a cabin in New Hampshire, right over the Massachusetts border. It was a quaint little place with a lovely fireplace, which they enjoyed in the cool of the evening. With limited funds at hand, Sylvia decided she had to find work somewhere in order to keep from sinking. She took a job as a waitress in a small restaurant, but there was very little business. She left that job and went to work a few hours in the evening in a diner. That seemed to work out better.

They stayed in New Hampshire about a month, and again, felt the need for someplace less expensive and closer to her home. Tony was now well enough for an occasional joyride to get him out into fresh air. They searched for a place in Massachusetts and found a cute cabin with cooking facilities in Ipswich, which they thought would do just fine. They purchased an electric skillet and saucepan, and she prepared all of the afternoon meals.

She would go to a local diner in the morning to purchase breakfast-to-go, and sometimes, as Tony continued to feel better, they would have breakfast together there. Their biggest meal was in the afternoon, prepared in the cabin. They would eat a light dinner out after she returned from feeding her children. Preparing the afternoon meals helped some financially. She couldn't possibly cook all three meals for him, go back and forth for her children, and work part time, too. The children made their own cereal in the morning. At lunch, she would purchase sandwiches, and she would prepare an early dinner for them.

One day, when she returned home at lunchtime to feed the children, Sylvia's daughter told her that a woman named Gingy was continually calling and asking for Sylvia. Tony had an older sister named Gingy, and Sylvia knew at once who her daughter was talking about.

Tony, at this point, was well enough to take the trips home with her. He would stay in the car while she tended to the children. One afternoon while she was at home, the phone rang. Her daughter answered it and informed Sylvia that it was that woman Gingy again. Sylvia took the phone and was asked if she knew where her brother Tony was. Finding out that he was just outside in the car, Gingy asked to speak with him. Sylvia went out to tell Tony his sister was on the phone, and asked if he wanted to speak to her. He agreed, knowing his family was very worried about him. When he hung up, he told Sylvia that his mother had purchased a new bed for him and wanted him to come home. He agreed.

He was well now, and to be truthful, Sylvia was a bit relieved. Soon, the children would be going back to school, and she desperately needed a full-time job in order to catch up on bills she had to let slide. Tony had paid two mortgage payments for her, but that was hardly sufficient.

This episode remains the most memorable series of events in the lives of Tony and Sylvia. Although initiated by a terrible health emergency, they always cherished the closeness, unity, and love they shared. It was a kind of love that neither had ever known before. Tony had a way of labeling things and, for some reason, would refer to the past few months as their "Everglades" experience. Also, during this time, Tony had mentioned marriage several times—but never actually proposed. Soon, their lives were to get a bit more complicated. Tony returned to his home to live.

Chapter 8

Tony's family consisted of three sisters and four brothers. Gingy, child number two, was ten years older than Tony. She was called upon to help her mother with the younger children. In their home, there was no tub or shower, and Gingy had the responsibility of washing her siblings with a washcloth. In fact, she continued this practice with her younger brothers until they reached puberty and started to get embarrassed. To others in the family circle, this really was not normal behavior.

Gingy was very controlling. Even after she got married and moved out, she maintained her hold on the rest of the family by going to her parents' home every day.

After many years of trying to have a child, she gave birth to a mongoloid girl. With this added burden and having no car, she would corral her family for help. Tony was called upon for everything that demanded transportation. He was always at her beck and call to go shopping, take her and the baby to the hospital or doctor's office or trips to the drug store, take them out on picnics, or even just a ride. Tony did this from the time he first got out of the hospital in 1952 until 1987.

There were three people in his family who had an uncanny control over him: his older sister Gingy, his brother Joe, and their aging mother. Tony's obligation, leading to being controlled, stemmed from several circumstances. After Gingy had her baby, she had a nervous breakdown. Her sister-in-law cared for the baby while Gingy was in the hospital.

Gingy also found out that she had contracted tuberculosis. Tony felt he was responsible, but the family made excuses such as the terrible apartment she had. He still felt he had to help in any way he could. Tony's older brother Joe also contracted TB, but in his case, since he was a bus driver, the family chose not to blame Tony. The argument was made that since Joe was in contact with so many other people, Tony could not be blamed. Still, Tony felt he was responsible.

Their aging mother also added to the guilt trip. Because she was no longer able to keep up with the household chores, Joe took on the cleaning and cooking, while Tony was made the maintenance man. He would do all of the electrical, plumbing, and carpentry work and resolve any other problem that would arise. He was, as mentioned previously, the full-time chauffeur for the family. He was also given the task of automobile mechanic. In the three-story walk-up, there was a married sister and a married brother, both with cars that Tony maintained. He also serviced his single brother's car all free of charge.

Tony was far too busy with these obligations; there was no further talk of marrying Sylvia. He did, however, become very close to Sylvia's family as they continued their relationship. Now that Ted and Sylvia were separated, Tony would drop by Sylvia's house each day while she was working. He would check on her children then pick her up at the train station each night. They would go for a ride so Sylvia could unwind from a hectic day, and then stop for a bite of dinner. Then they would spend the rest of the night together until he left for home about 11:00 PM. This continued from 1960 through 1969.

Although on the surface, everything seemed all right, and they were still very much in love, Sylvia could not see any chance that the relationship would culminate in marriage.

But it must be said that Tony not only cared for her children while she was at work, he took Sylvia and her sister shopping each weekend, and on many family rides. Many times he took them to Salem Willows where the children could go on amusements. Sometimes he would go fishing, bring the catch to Sylvia's, prepare and serve, and clean up. He was now doing for Sylvia in the same way he did for his family.

Sylvia's youngest child, Dan, will tell you that Tony was the only father he had ever known. Not only did he see Tony as a father figure, he was their protector as well.

One time, Sylvia and Tony returned home to find Dan very ill. Her children had been told never to call Sylvia at work unless it was an emergency. It was, but Dan never called. He spent the entire day on the couch with a high fever and very upset stomach. When they saw Dan's condition, Sylvia called the doctor, who instructed her to get Dan to him as quickly as possible. Tony quickly wrapped Dan in a blanket and they rocketed out the door. When they reached the doctor's office, Tony again took charge of getting Dan out of the car and into the office. Dan was dehydrated from vomiting all day and began convulsing. This worried Tony and Sylvia even more. With fluids and some medication, however, Dan was soon back on his feet. Tony had stepped up, and Dan never forgot it.

At this time, Sylvia's husband had yet another girlfriend. Ted wanted to take his children and the girlfriend out on the weekend. Lynda and Teddie Junior had gone once, but reported to Sylvia that he had taken them on a picnic with a case of beer in his trunk. Ted's drinking bothered the kids, and infuriated Sylvia. They were never allowed to go with Ted again.

There was a final time that involved Dan. One Saturday, Ted appeared at the door and was after Dan. Lynda and Teddie Junior, being older than Dan, had already made up their minds about not going with their father. Sylvia refused to let Dan go, but Ted grabbed him by the arm. Sylvia grabbed his other arm. They actually had a tug-of-war with Dan in the middle.

Tony was upstairs resting, and Sylvia cried out to him for help. Tony ran down the stairs and grabbed Dan from Ted and gave him to Sylvia. He then proceeded to beat Ted while pushing him out the door. Ted was bruised and bleeding by the time Tony was done. Tony screamed, "Get out of here and don't come back or I'll kill you." Thoroughly trounced, Ted never did come back. Dan felt very secure, knowing Tony would protect him.

On Dan's seventh birthday, his birthday was August 30. Tony took Sylvia and Dan to Salem Willows. Much to their surprise, they were having an end-of-season special. For fifty cents, Tony bought a ticket that let Dan ride every ride multiple times all day. Dan never forgot that day.

After having been separated for a year and a half, their twelve and a half years of marriage ended. Sylvia divorced Ted. She was immediately faced with all of the expenses of a family. The multiple burdens of mortgage payments, utilities, and, of course, food for the struggling family were now squarely on her shoulders.

Her work as an adult had always been as an executive secretary, but she found the $50.00 to $75.00 a week was woefully inadequate. A neighbor, knowing of her struggles, told her of an opening at a local meat-packing plant that paid $90.00 a week. Overtime was available for even more money. The neighbor spoke with the owner of the company on her behalf, and she got an interview.

Seeing how pretty she was and noting her work experience to date, the owner went out of his way to explain the poor conditions and unpleasantness of the job. It was because of this that the job paid so well. But, undaunted, Sylvia took the job. Her soon-to-be co-workers were told that a secretary was going to start in two weeks. (Sylvia wanted to give her then current employer proper notice.) For some reason, during those two weeks, the factory workers' animosity grew so much that from the very first day, Sylvia was treated with a good deal of hostility. They did everything they could to make her life miserable.

Her job was working on a conveyor belt in a huge freezer. It was simple enough, but, being the newest employee, Sylvia was put at the beginning of the line. The first person was expected to pack the largest number of five-pound boxes. The most senior employee, at the end of the line, with little else to do, would constantly yell at Sylvia that she was not packing enough. This went on continuously for four and a half years. Sylvia packed and cried the whole time, but remember, she's Sicilian – tough as nails. She did not give up.

Her one friend worked at the end of the line and would weigh each box, adding or subtracting hot dogs as needed, to make the required five pounds. After about six months, he approached Sylvia during a break, saying that he was aware that the shift foreman, Teddie, needed some help. Teddie had to calculate the loss of weight of the smoked shoulders and hams after being smoked. The meats were injected with water to add weight. If they stayed in the smoke house too long, they would lose too much water—an unacceptable situation.

Teddie had to keep a quality control sheet, calculating the loss of weight. He was not much of a mathematician, and had a great deal of difficulty with it.

He was elated that Sylvia was interested in helping out. After a short instructional session, once a week, Sylvia would be relieved from packing hotdogs at about 2:00 P.M. to perform her new duties.

This only made matters worse with the other workers on the hot dog line. It was so bad, she couldn't stay in the factory during her lunch hour. She would go the nearby library every day and chose to read instructional books on floral design. She actually taught herself a profession that would be very handy later in her life.

Chapter 9

October 5, 1963 was Sylvia's birthday. Tony, as usual, picked her up at the train station after she got out of work at the meatpacking plant.

Since Tony's family was so large and nearly always in tight financial situations, birthdays of his family members were never observed. In fact, in most cases, the children didn't even know when the others were born. The exceptions were the first three children. They seemed to know almost everything about the family history.

So it was that Tony never celebrated anyone's birthday—including Sylvia's. Other than her sixteenth birthday party that her parents held, Tony never acknowledged her birthday over the many years he had known her. It sort of bothered Sylvia, but she never said anything. This time, things were to be a bit different.

Now in Tony's car after a hard day's work, they took their usual ride, this time to the Lynn/Nahant shore. Tony thought he would stop and see if Lenny was around. He was a sixteen-year-old boy Tony had befriended during his many fishing trips to the area. Lenny had a skiff in which the two would spend a good deal of time out in the harbor. Tony parked the car in the lot of an ice-cream parlor and went off to find his friend. Lenny was not only around, he was nearby, out on the water in his skiff (just as Tony had arranged). Tony returned to the car and asked Sylvia if it would be all right to go with Lenny just to see if the fish were biting. He assured her that he would not be long. That was fine with her.

There was Sylvia, stuck waiting in the car. And she waited and waited. She thought that this was no way to spend a birthday. After what must have been two or three hours, she finally got out of the car and entered the parlor for some ice cream. She noticed there was a little girl's birthday party going on.

When she was seated, she noticed a card on the table, stating that if it was your birthday, you would get a free sundae. She asked the waitress if the policy applied to all ages, and it did. It was her birthday, and Sylvia was not to be denied at least something festive. She ordered a hot fudge sundae and sat, still quite alone, and tried to enjoy it.

The children's party finally broke up and Sylvia thought she had better get back to the car. Again, she waited. About a half hour later, she saw Tony approaching. He was carrying a very large cardboard box and grinning from ear to ear, proudly stating that he had caught thirty six flounders. Sylvia was boiling. It was like he thought he had been gone only fifteen minutes. He put the box in the trunk, got in the car, and headed home. Sylvia kept quiet the entire trip, just stewing at Tony's lack of care.

When they got back to the house, Tony put the box of flounder on the kitchen table. Sylvia could hold out for only a couple of minutes more. She opened the door, picked up the box, and tossed it outside, and bellowed, "Pick up your fish and get out of here." Tony was shocked. She told him it was her birthday and she had spent it alone, in a car, while he went fishing.

Tony was afraid to go back. After a few days he had his brother George call to see if Sylvia had cooled off. Of course, by that time she had, and Tony returned, taking up their usual routine as if nothing had happened.

One thing did happen, though: Tony never forgot another birthday, and bought her a large, beautiful, and loving birthday card each year.

Coincidently, Sylvia went to visit his sister and there was his brother Sam. In the course of the conversation, Sam asked Sylvia when was her birthday? She replied, "October 5th." This was very coincidental since it was immediately after the birthday tiff with Tony. Sam must have heard about it. With that Sam replied, "That's my father's birthday."

The next time Sylvia saw Tony, she told him of the conversation. The following October, Tony bought a simple but decorated birthday cake for his father. When he noticed the cake on the table, his father asked, what was the cake for. The fact it was his birthday didn't impress him. Neither did the cake. He just shrugged his shoulders and walked away. It was the first and last cake Tony would buy him.

At one point, a new packer was hired and took the obligatory place at the beginning of the line. Having been through the same thing, Sylvia felt an immediate affinity for Susan, and they became casual friends. They would have lunch at a neighborhood restaurant. One of the restaurant's owners had a sister who bred German shepherds, one of which had just had a litter of pups. Sylvia bought one as a high school graduation present for her daughter, who named him Dane.

Dane grew very quickly, and it soon became apparent that his appetite needed curbing. But, as happens in many families, Dane was to commit a major transgression. Sylvia had cooked a pot roast. She placed it on their table, and went into the living room, where her children were watching television. She wanted the children to finish the show, so she sat with her children. She knew the show would be over shortly. Dane had his opportunity! When the family went back to the kitchen, he was sitting by the table with a very contented look on his face. There was not a trace of the pot roast.

Tony loved Dane, and they would play together many times. At one point, Tony noticed a string in Dane's mouth. Gathering him up, Tony pulled that string, and pulled, and pulled! It became obvious that the ravenous pup had swallowed a whole spool of string. Cats will play with a ball of string; Dane ate his!

One day, Sylvia invited Susan to her home. They both had children about the same age, and it seemed to be a perfect match. Susan, however, was a very promiscuous woman—and Tony, on that day, was there. She was obviously attracted to Tony, and asked where he lived. Sylvia, being very naive, told her, creating another opportunity for Tony to roam. It wasn't long before Susan contacted him and set up a date. Tony had no intention of seriously considering her for any lasting relationship, but like most men, would take a woman up on any offer. While most unmarried men wouldn't care, Tony would be sorry for it later.

With her seemingly incredible memory, Sylvia knew it happened on a Wednesday when she was working in the office. She decided to call Tony. His brother answered the phone, and said that Tony had been out all day. Reality set in for her like a bolt of lightning. Susan had called in sick that day. This happened two times that Sylvia was aware of. The third time, Sylvia called Tony once again. He had not left the house yet, and she just kept talking, but never accused him of anything. Tony got the hint. He finally said,"Syl, I'm not going out, I'm staying home." Triumph? Yes! But the hurt to Sylvia remained for many months beyond, despite Tony's attempts at gaining redemption.

At a local restaurant, they were both impressed by the unique construction of the ceiling. Instead of plaster or tile, it had boards, about four inches apart, nailed to the beams of the ceiling. Each was sculpted and had small lights and artificial grapes dangling from it. Sylvia thought such a design would work well in her basement. Soon after, in true Tony style (in yet another attempt at redemption for the Susan affair), he took her to a lumberyard, where she picked out the wood for the basement project. With the rough-hewn wood needing much work, Tony purchased a jigsaw to sculpt the edges of the rough-hewn wood from Sears. Having an unconditional guarantee on its tools, the store, with some regret, replaced four saws during Tony's construction project. It was, for Sears, a nightmare, but for Tony, it was yet another labor of love.

As chilling as her hot-dog experience was, Sylvia never lost sight of her true skill set. Finding that office salaries had improved over the years to near her meatpacking pay, she opted to leave the meatpacking business and re-enter office life. She left without telling a soul, and gave no notice.

Her next office job, even though she was out of the market for those four and a half years, was with Schrafft's Chocolate, as head of accounts payable. She was in charge of all expenses, including payroll. Schrafft's, however, was already on its last legs. A daughter of the founders put the final dagger into the company. She hired a lawyer to run the company but he did so to his own advantage. He changed the recipes to an inferior quality but maintained the same prices. With the holidays approaching, he created a sales incentive. If customers paid for their candy orders before the holidays, they could do so at a greatly discounted price. It worked. He knew the company was to be sold to Bachman-Jax and when Bachman-Jax took over, they soon discovered they had to fill orders for which they had not, and would not receive any payment. They filled and shipped the orders anyway. Sylvia was given a lot of overtime pulling invoices for those orders to be presented to the court as there was a lawsuit now in progress. The overtime pay helped her considerably but the company soon died a corporate death.

Sylvia then contacted an employment agency in search of a new job. Ironically they sent her to McKesson Liquor, a major distributor in New England. Sylvia had worked for the company between her junior and senior year of high school. With only two months before her senior year, and with all intentions of graduating, she looked for and applied for a permanent full-time position. She interviewed with an elderly gentleman who was the office manager, and got a job in accounts receivable recording sales figures. By summer's end, she had to come up with a plausible story for her boss. She claimed that her father insisted that she go to business school, and she left McKesson for her senior year of high school.

The second time around at McKesson, Sylvia was now thirty-nine and her children were twenty, nineteen, and fifteen. When she re-contacted McKesson's, she was surprised to find the same gentleman with whom she had first interviewed. Now in his eighties, he again instantly took to Sylvia. Evidently, he was not concerned (or did not remember) how she left the company years before.

After a few months, the gentleman called Sylvia to his office one Friday. Having been called out of retirement and rehired by McKesson as a consultant, his intent now was to rid the company of a poorly performing office manager. He had hired Sylvia with this intent all along, but wanted to observe her skills and demeanor for those few months. Now, convinced she was the woman for the job, Sylvia was told that he had let the office manager go, and, beginning the following Monday, he would train her in her new duties. She would be responsible for three men and four other women in the office.

During those few months, every day, the consultant would arrive at work at 8:30 AM for the opening of the office at 9:00. On that Monday, Sylvia arrived at about 8:45, but he wasn't there. She had the position, but who was to train her? At 9:00, she received a call from the consultant's wife. It seems her husband had a massive heart attack, passed away, and, obviously, would not be in to work.

Sylvia and the rest of the office staff attended the funeral. The next day, the men of the office contacted the owners, requesting that a man be transferred from their Connecticut office to Boston to be the new office manager. The transfer happened, leaving Sylvia disappointed and without the promotion she was counting on.

Chapter 10

It was now nearing the end of July 1969, and it was time to start looking for yet another job. She contacted, in person, an employment agency in Boston. The receptionist accepted Sylvia's résumé and assigned her to Ken, a rather young man, to act as her counselor. His inexperience was rather obvious. He had no clue what to do with a thirty-nine-year-old woman. Soon, the manager of the agency got involved, read her résumé, and found her to be very well qualified for several positions at various clients the agency was representing.

While she was still at McKesson, Sylvia would talk with Ken at the agency during her lunch hour. The transferred office manager got the drift of what she was up to and contacted the same agency in hopes of finding her replacement. After a few weeks, Sylvia was placed with a law firm as an accountant for the twenty-six attorneys in the office. She had given a proper two-week notice and found out later that three women were hired to replace her. Although she was asked to stay at McKesson, the new position offered a considerable amount of money more than she was getting. Sylvia had decided she really wanted to leave McKesson, and even an offered raise to match her new position's pay was not enough to change her mind.

After the law office hired Sylvia, Ken contacted her. It seems that the manager of the agency, whose name was Richard, had more than assisted her in getting employed, he had really noticed her. Ken was acting as a broker of another sort. Richard (or Rick to his friends) wanted a date. Sylvia wondered why Rick couldn't speak for himself. She told Ken that she was already seeing someone else. Rick, however, was persistent, and had Ken call again the next day.

All Rick wanted was to meet after work for a drink. Sylvia had been caring for Tony for ten years with never a mention of marriage. She thought there was no transgression in the offing, and agreed to meet with Rick. She told Tony she had a lot of work to do, and she would call him when she was ready to be picked up.

During a pleasant conversation with Rick, Sylvia chose a sweet, pleasant-tasting drink. She was not a drinker, but the Brandy Alexander was tolerable. That first meeting lasted all of forty-five minutes. The following day, Ken called again, and again she accepted. This time, Rick talked so long that Sylvia ordered a second drink. On the third meeting, Rick told Sylvia he had broken a six-year-long affair with another woman. Sylvia was stunned. She couldn't believe he would leave someone so abruptly after six years. He talked so long, Sylvia ended up having three drinks on an empty stomach. It was Friday, and as was custom, Tony picked her up and they went to Sylvia's sister's home. A couple of blocks from the house, the drinks and lack of food caught up with her. Tony pulled over for her. Although the smell of alcohol was prominent, Tony never said a word. Eventually, they arrived at her sister's home, where she was made a sandwich that seemed to settle her stomach.

A few days later, it was time for a confrontation with Tony. She wanted him to tell his family of their current relationship within a week, but after only a few days she figured he was not going to do so. She asked him if he had complied. Even though he said he had, she knew he was lying. If his family had been told, the next obvious step would have been to take her to meet with them.

Tony – In his room and lonely

When Tony next picked her up, upon arriving at her home, she told Tony she was leaving him. With not another word spoken, he quietly left, stunned. He had never imagined their relationship would end, it was now the second week of August of 1969.

The next day, she told Rick of the breakup, and a new relationship began. Rick lived in Boston, and they both worked in Boston. It was convenient to meet for breakfast, lunch, and dinner each day. At one point, Rick asked her what she would like to do in the evening after dinner. She loved to go dancing but hadn't gone for twenty years. That was enough for Rick, and dancing was added to the daily routine. Rick told Sylvia that he had been an altar boy during his youth. Sylvia knew that Boston's Saint Anthony's Church would hold a Mass every twenty minutes throughout the day for shoppers and workers alike. Attending Mass was added to their lunchtime routine.

After two weeks of seeing each other continuously, Rick contacted his brother Gus, and invited him to join them for lunch. She was flattered that Gus and his wife invited them for a Sunday dinner. His wife went out of her way to prepare and serve a four-course meal. Sylvia was very impressed, but thought about the invitation again. She had been seeing Tony for twenty years. After her teens, Tony had never taken her home to his family again. Rick, after only two weeks, was more than proud to take her to meet his family. What a contrast. She was pleased at the way this relationship was developing. Sylvia's children, on the other hand, did not adjust to the changes immediately.

During this time, Sylvia's daughter, as well as her sons, saw no reason to sever their relationships with Tony. He had taken on the role of father for the past ten years, and there was a strong bond among them. Sylvia's daughter Lynda was now twenty-two years of age and married. She now had sole possession of Dane the dog. She, her husband, and Dane lived in the basement apartment in her father's house in East Boston, where Tony also lived.

One day, Lynda took Dane for a walk. Suddenly, Dane took off. She couldn't imagine what was wrong with him. When she began to run after him, she realized where he was going. He had scented Tony, and quickly jumped all over him. Tony was very surprised to see him. Tony was taking his mother to a clinic for some reason. The clinic was in the center of the city, near a park, and that was where Lynda was headed with Dane. Tony's mother didn't know what in the world was going on. Tony explained to his mother that the girl was Sylvia's daughter.

After this chance meeting, Lynda began inviting Tony to her home on Saturdays. He would arrive around 11:00 in the morning and stay until 11:00 at night. Lynda would discuss much of what was going on in Sylvia's life and her relationship with Rick.

As for Teddie Junior, he (at first) resented Tony and gave him a difficult time. So Tony cooled it with Teddie for a period of time. As Rick entered the picture and Sylvia broke up with Tony, Teddie would call Tony, crying and asking if he was the reason for the Tony-Sylvia breakup. Tony assured him that was not the case in any way, shape, or form. Every so often, Tony would take him out for a game of billiards. Son Dan also kept in touch.

When Sylvia left Tony, she honestly felt that she would be freeing him to lead a life free of bonds and that he would take full advantage of it. In later years, she was to find out that exactly the opposite occurred. For the most part of the next seventeen and a half years (during the time Sylvia was married to Rick) Tony stayed very close to home, with the exception of the Saturday visits to Lynda's house. On weekday evenings, after dinner, he would take a ride to the mall and walk or sit at the food court until 8:30 and would be home by 9:00 PM. He would watch a movie and retire for the night.

On one of Tony's visits with Lynda he was told that her mother and Rick frequented the local dog track. Tony suggested to his two bachelor brothers that they go to the track. They agreed, not really knowing why he wanted to go. His hope was that he might see Sylvia. Sylvia and Rick, however, were in the clubhouse. Tony and his brothers were in the grandstand. When Lynda told him that her mother and Rick had stopped going to the track, Tony stopped going. Tony obviously missed Sylvia rather badly,

With her children grown, Sylvia thought she would sell her little Cape Cod-style home and get something different. She had even gone so far as to train for and obtain a real-estate license. Tony had always opposed the idea of her selling her home. He lived only ten minutes from Sylvia; it was a matter of convenience for him.

Rick, on the other hand, thought it would be a great idea, and was all for it. He even started painting the interior from top to bottom. During her meatpacking days, Sylvia had new siding put on and the house was ready to go on the market.

They were married in December of 1969, and started looking for a new home. They found a large Victorian in Brookline. On January 1, 1970, a new year was beginning just as Rick and Sylvia were beginning new lives together. On that very day, they moved into their new home.

At one point, Lynda told Sylvia that Tony was interested in getting back together. He wished Sylvia would leave her new husband. But Sylvia saw a very good side of Rick. He was extremely loyal and sensitive. Inwardly, she knew she had to see this relationship through and wrote the following to Tony:

March 30, 1970
Dear T.M.,

I am truly sorry for what has happened to us, but I can't possibly see how I can turn back now.

I was harboring so much hurt, at the fact that you didn't want to marry me, and that your family wouldn't accept me. Also the fact that you wanted me to stay away from them, that I felt you and they were ashamed of me and I couldn't live that way.

I really think this is the best for the both of us.

Goodbye,
Sylvia

(Note that in the salutation, Tony was referred to as T.M. It was a nickname given him by some of his friends.)

Now that her children were grown and living their own lives, Sylvia entertained the idea of someday having a shelter for the elderly. Instead of leading an inactive life full of despair, she thought she would like to help keep them active, with social activities and the like. But as time went on, financial problems began to emerge. They had all they could do just to keep their heads above water. Thoughts of pursuing her dream had to be put aside. It was not God's timing.

Within a matter of months, other factors started shaping their relationship. Among them, Rick's employment agency entered bankruptcy. He was now forty-four, and for most good jobs, the phrase "overqualified" kept popping up. He found it very difficult to find meaningful employment.

While working at her various office positions, Sylvia had taken advantage of her self-taught floral design skills. She would bring in beautiful floral arrangements. Women in the offices liked them so much, they would ask her to make specific ones to their liking, and bought them from her.

With Rick now unemployed, he suggested they go into the floral business together. He had gone to college in Chicago and New York State University, and majored in marketing, advertising, and public relations. He asked Sylvia in what field of floristry she had particular interest. He was really going to get into this new venture with a passion. The two decided to focus on doing wedding designs.

Rick started looking in the classifieds and engagement announcements in several metropolitan papers. He had already decided that by doing custom designs for weddings, he and Sylvia could work right out of their house. They devoted two rooms to the new business. He would pick and choose prospective clients very carefully, calling them to explain how they could take a large burden out of planning a wedding. With a portfolio of designs for ideas, they would meet with the clients and banter ideas back and forth, helping the client design their wedding flowers.

Rick also asked Sylvia to teach him how to prepare the flowers, so that most of her job was designing the bouquets, centerpieces, and church sprays. He learned to wire and tape flowers, and to dye them to match the gowns. As he prepared the flowers, Sylvia would put them all together. They were quite the team and for four and a half years, the business thrived. Well, not quite. What Sylvia and Rick had not really thought about was the seasonality of weddings. Very few weddings take place during the cold New England winters. They were always struggling to make enough money to carry them over those winter months.

But the springs and summers were a different story. They would book as many as seven weddings on the weekends. Starting with one on a Friday night, they would book three on Saturday and three on Sunday. They really had to spend twenty-three hours a day to accomplish the work. To take advantage of the freshness of the flowers, the process started early Wednesday with a trip to the Boston flower market. Then, working side by side, the grueling schedule would not stop until the last delivery was made on Sunday. With the frenzied activity over, their hours reversed. They would sleep very late on Mondays and Tuesdays before the mad rush began again on Wednesday.

One time, Rick got a virus. He was very ill and could not participate with Sunday's deliveries. The last delivery was in Lowell, a city thirty miles northwest of Boston. Sylvia had to make that run alone. With the flowers delivered, she went to another client's home to pick up their payment for the following weekend wedding. Sylvia would always demand the flowers be paid for in advance. She had gotten burned a couple of times when the business first started.

Since she had only three hours of sleep in as many days, Sylvia was exhausted. When she arrived at her last stop, the mother of the bride took one look at her and knew she was about dead on her feet. She made Sylvia a cup of tea and a sandwich, and they had a nice, relaxing social hour. She then collected the payment and left Lowell for home in Beverly.

It was a combination of exhaustion, the warm tea, and the relief that the weekend was over that got Sylvia into a bit of trouble. She was on Route 62 in Danvers that late Sunday afternoon when she became extremely tired, and put her head against the car window and fell asleep. Luckily, the road was nearly devoid of traffic due to the day and hour. She did not lose control, but with the weight of her foot on the gas pedal, her speed increased. Her left hand, also weighted with sleep, caused her car to veer slowly to the left.

As she approached an intersection, she heard three very loud knocks on the window where her head was lolling. The knocks startled her awake. She estimates she was going about 70 miles per hour. She looked to the left and a figure was there. It was a man who was nicely dressed, in a suit. He was of medium build and perhaps five foot eight. As she watched, he walked toward the back of the car, around to the trunk, and disappeared.

Rick – After delivering flowers for a wedding

Coming back to reality, she realized she was over to the furthest left of the roadway, facing oncoming traffic. She was headed directly for a Ford pickup truck. The driver was horrified and gripped his steering wheel, bracing for the inevitable impact. Sylvia managed to regain control of her car and scooted into her own lane, shaking from the experience.

About a week earlier, she had a conversation involving a book her daughter had read about angels. At the time, Sylvia thought to herself that the contents of that book were outrageous. After the incident with the man, the pickup truck, and her narrow escape, she never doubted the existence of angels again.

It was now the mid 1970s. During the trips taken to visit clients, purchase flowers, and deliver them, Rick was the passenger as Sylvia drove. He liked to listen to radio evangelists, and his early religious upbringing began to re-emerge.

After four and a half years of floral designing, Sylvia and Rick were forced to quit because of one very bad winter. After always teetering on financial ruin during the off-season, one storm put them down. They had purchased and prepared flowers for their own bridal show in Haverhill, and the storm hit. It was so bad, virtually no one could get to the show. Traveling over solidly iced roads, they finally made it, but all was lost. With very few attending the show, the cost of the flowers and all the time and effort spent was to no avail.

Things got so bad that they found it difficult, if not impossible, to make payments on their company van. Inevitably, they left the house to go to a future customer's home and ... no van. It had been repossessed. Now they were stranded in Amesbury and were virtually out of business.

Sylvia looking at this strange set of circumstances felt that perhaps it was a blessing in disguise. They had worked so hard for years and here was an opportunity to stop, rest and re-evaluate where they were going.

Chapter 11

Rick got a job as a maintenance supervisor for a large apartment complex, which included an apartment for them at no cost. On New Year's Eve that year, a tenant—drunk and angry with the landlord—proceeded to try to burn down one of the buildings. Repairing the damage done gave Rick a job for quite some time. They had to swallow their pride, however, and ask for public assistance. They received food stamps valued at $70.00 a month.

After the fire damage was repaired, Rick found another complex that needed his talents. It was a beautiful series of buildings set in a forest. Trees had been hewn to make room for the complex, but many were still standing, and made for a marvelous picnic area. Picnic tables, barbecue pits, and a wonderful in-ground pool rounded out the scene.

Sylvia was used to having her family over for Mother's Day and Christmas each year, but being in this financial bind, the practice had been suspended for the last several years. With the 1979 Fourth of July approaching, Sylvia and Rick planned on a big family cookout. The food stamps provided everything they needed. In the past, it was tradition to have guests return home with some leftovers, but not this year. Sylvia realized the leftovers would have to stay to make it through the month.

Sometimes, God allows hardship and lets His people reach rock bottom so that He can then pick them up to the heights He has in mind for them. The picnic went very well. The family had a good time and Sylvia was pleased. The following day, with only $10.00 in food stamps left to their name, Sylvia and Rick walked to a local store. They never argued about money. However, Rick was concerned about the lack of it. He asked, "Sylvia, how many food stamps do we have left?" She replied, "Ten dollars – Don't worry, God will provide."

No sooner did those words come from her mouth than she noticed what appeared to be Monopoly money on the ground. Sylvia walked past it, but something inside her made her walk back to examine the object. When she stooped down and picked it up she saw it was seven ten-dollar bills, folded in half, and so new and crisp it seemed they had just gotten off the press. Seventy dollars was exactly what they needed to survive the month. Another gift from God!

In the meantime, a woman heard of their plight, and, in 1980, found a job for Sylvia in the office of the Newburyport Redevelopment Authority. The downtown area was being completely dressed up and renovated to draw tourists to the town. This woman went out of her way to take Sylvia to work every morning and back every night for a few weeks, because Sylvia had no means of transportation. God also provided angels to accomplish what was needed

After a few weeks, another girl was hired. She had been given the family car, but for some reason, was not using it. She sold the car to Sylvia for a mere $50.00, payable in two installments. Again God's provision was evident.

Now that Rick and Sylvia had their evenings to themselves, with no flowers to accompany them, they started watching TV together. Rick found The 700 Club, a Christian program run by Pat Robertson, a TV evangelist. They enjoyed the show very much. At the end of each show, Robertson would ask all in his audience, and at home to repeat a prayer after him. It is what Christians call "The Sinner's Prayer." In essence, what is said is:-

"Dear God, please forgive me of all of my sins. I give myself to You and ask You to come into my life and guide me and protect me. I will turn my life of sin over to you and ask for your forgiveness. From this day on I will live only for You."

At the end of each show, every night, Sylvia and Rick held hands and repeated the prayer. This is what Christians call being "born again." The prayer need be said only once, but with their Catholic background (where one repeated the telling of sins each and every time in church), they felt the same applied. So for three years, they gained redemption, far beyond their need.

Sylvia again had the feeling she would like to have a shelter, this time for hard-to-place orphans. Adopters generally like to adopt infants, and there were so many children too old for most prospective parents. This also was not God's timing. Because they continued to struggle financially, it was not feasible.

Now that Sylvia had a car, she began looking for work in the Boston area. She found an accountant's position in a tie-manufacturing plant. They also found yet another apartment complex in Malden, a suburb of Boston. Rick was hired as the maintenance supervisor, and the two lived, once again, rent-free.

In 1982, while at work, Sylvia received a phone call from the hospital. Rick had a heart attack and was taken there. She quickly left work to be with her husband. He survived the attack, but with too much of a diminished ability to continue as a maintenance supervisor. For the next two years, Sylvia supported the household.

They moved to Everett, another Boston suburb, and took up residence on the second floor of a standard old two-family house. Rick was put on disability, Sylvia's employer went bankrupt—and the struggle continued. She got a job with a vitamin manufacturer in Cambridge (yes, another Boston suburb–there's a lot of them), as an accountant.

Rick didn't like staying home all alone in the six-room apartment, so he would take her to work, occupy himself until their lunchtime get-together, and busy himself again until he picked her up at the end of the day. They would dine out and then go home together.

At this point, Sylvia's Lynda had a son named Christopher. Born in October of 1980, he was now three years of age. Rick and Sylvia or Lynda's mother-in-law would be asked to baby-sit. Lynda was still having Tony over every Saturday, and Christopher loved him, calling him his friend.

It was a family tradition that every Sunday, dinner was at Sylvia's parent's home. Sylvia, Rick, her sister Lydia and all of the grandchildren, their spouses, and now Christopher, would congregate over the dinner meal, and fellowship together. In conversations during the meal, little Christopher would talk about Tony incessantly. Every time Christopher would tell a story about Tony, he would always begin with, "My friend Tony" this or "My friend Tony that. No one asked who this Tony was because they all knew.

Now that she was living in West Roxbury, Sylvia and Rick would spontaneously go to visit Lynda and her husband on Saturday, because Lynda was working during the week. They were cordial, but Sylvia always thought there was something else going on. She would feel like she and Rick were getting the bum's rush. What they didn't know was that Tony was there. Lynda would rush Tony out the back door until Sylvia and Rick left.

One time, however, their usual visit took a different turn. Lynda took longer than usual to answer the door, and invited Sylvia in, alone. Lynda didn't know what to do. Tony had had enough of his back-door exits. He now refused to leave. Lynda said, Mom, Tony is here and he won't leave. Sylvia suggested Lynda could introduce Tony to Rick and Sylvia as Joe, a friend of Lynda's husband. She got Rick from outside and proceeded to walk into the living room. The introductions were made, but Sylvia felt very uneasy, and knew things were going to get ugly.

Tony, Lynda and family had been watching TV when Sylvia and Rick arrived. Sylvia, for a lack of anything to say, simply asked, "What are you watching?" With that Tony used this, to affirm himself. He was going to let Rick know that he knew Sylvia. Tony looked directly at Sylvia and said, "It's The Honeymooners, don't you remember?" With that being said, Sylvia made her excuses, took Rick by arm and left.

As soon as they were back in the car, Rick questioned her about the stranger. Sylvia tried to bolster the "Joe Story," but Rick was having none of it. Rick told Sylvia he didn't believe that was Paul's friend. There was approximately, over twenty years difference in age. Beside, Rick had deduced that since Paul came from Needham, and the stranger spoke with a solid East Boston accent, he had to be Tony.

Sylvia knew well that an argument would develop. She slammed the door on any further conversation about Joe. Rick was a very jealous man, but could control it, except, when it came to Tony, the mere mention of his name bothered him tremendously.

Chapter 12

Problems continued to arise for the couple. In 1984, Rick told Sylvia that he thought he had some kind of virus. He needed to go to the hospital to get it checked out. He did not mention that he had noticed blood in his stool. The doctor made a diagnosis of colon cancer and soon operated. A portion of Rick's colon was removed. The first six-month follow-up exam discovered no problems, but after a year, Rick was told the cancer had indeed returned, and spread.

Another operation was scheduled and completed, but this time, there were complications. There was some seepage of fluid from the incision. On morning rounds the next day, with a gaggle of residents in tow, Rick's doctor reviewed his case and asked for opinions as to what to do next. One doctor suggested the application of a hydrocollator pack and the head doctor agreed.

Hydrocollator packs warm tissue by conduction. Packs are immersed in a hot water bath, removed from the bath when needed, wrapped in six to eight layers of toweling for an insulating cover, and are then applied to the patient. To avoid scalding, the covering towels or pack should have been checked for excessive heat.

A nurse was assigned the task. There were two major problems, however. The head doctor and the doctor who made the recommendation had never seen such a pack applied. The nurse, employed for only six months, had been shown the procedure during her first week. She never touched one again and had completely forgotten how the procedure was done. She laid one thin towel over Rick's incision and applied an all-too-hot hydrocollator pack.

Rick had another nurse, a former Catholic priest, who came on duty at the shift change. He had been stationed in Africa, where he contracted some sort of liver problem. He resigned, married, and became a nurse. When he removed the dressing, Sylvia was there and he called her over to view a gruesome sight. Rick, thankfully, was heavily sedated with morphine and never felt a thing, but when removed, the pack had scalded a five-inch by nine-inch hole over his abdomen. She could actually see Rick's belly fat boiling.

The nurse suggested she photograph the wound, and she rushed home to get her camera. When she returned to Rick's side, the nurse again removed the dressing, walked out of the room, and closed the door behind him. Sylvia took picture after picture. She took shots to show the location of the wound, and close-ups to show the severity of it. When she finished, she called the nurse back in to re-bandage the wound.

That evening, at home and watching The 700 Club, she called in for prayer she was so upset. A gracious woman was told what had transpired with Rick and she asked if Sylvia had a local church she was attending. Sylvia explained she was raised a Catholic, but was not going to any particular church at the time. The woman asked if she could refer Sylvia to a local, spirit filled church. At this point, Sylvia was open to and welcomed any and all suggestions and noted the name and address of the church nearest home.

The male nurse cared for Rick very well. About three times every day, he would clean the burn so it would not get infected. But even with this care, Rick stayed in the hospital much longer than expected. During this time, Rick and Sylvia were told that his illness was terminal. His liver was now also infected with cancer. The doctors gave him two years to live. When he finally went home, the burn had not completely healed. Sylvia tended to it, following the instructions of the male nurse, until it was finally and completely healed.

On the second day after Rick's release from the hospital, the doorbell rang. The visitor was a woman whose church had been contacted by the 700 Club. She asked if she may talk to both of them, and both agreed. Rick and Sylvia felt they needed all of the spiritual contact they could get.

The woman explained how she was given their names more than a month ago, and she had intended to visit. However, because the church had no means of transportation for those who needed it, the task was impossible. After that month, she realized she still had their name and address in her pocket. Something told her to follow up. Sylvia explained, had she tried to contact them earlier, she would not have found them. Both were spending a good deal of time in the hospital every day.

God always has His perfect timing. The church their visitor represented was Glad Tidings, a Pentecostal Church in Everett. Based in an old converted theatre, the church became theirs. They were both baptized there. For both of them, it was a wonderful experience.

As time went on, Sylvia went in search of a lawyer in the Boston Yellow Pages. Spying a half-page ad, she figured that anyone who could afford such an ad must be successful. She called, made an appointment, and took with her the array of photos she had taken. The photos were so vivid, the attorney took the case. However, it took nearly a year before the case went to court.

Sylvia's youngest son Dan had put himself through college, and married. As time went on he had a daughter, born July 21, 1986. When he graduated with his MBA, his daughter was in his arms.

Continuing her search for a life's calling, Sylvia wrote another evangelist by the name of Robert Schuller. In the letter, she related her idea for a home for hard-to-place orphans, and asked for the name of Schuller's architect and advertising agency. He wrote back in a week, saying his architect had passed away. He gave his name anyway. The advertising agency was a Madison Avenue firm in New York.

Sylvia followed up by writing the agency, relating her contact with Schuller, and asking for any advice they might offer. They wrote back very politely, but in essence, told her to contact them again when she had more to work with. But they did ask a few interesting questions: Did she have a board of directors? Did she have non-profit status with the government, as a 501©3 organization? These two questions in particular would give Sylvia a starting point later.

Rick's court case lasted all of three days, though it was scheduled for a week. The pictures she had taken were so vivid, the hospital didn't have a leg to stand on. The defense kept repeating that Rick was terminally ill (as if that helped their case). They were very cruel.

On the second day of the trial, the attorneys pulled Rick and Sylvia aside to discuss a settlement. Their first offer was $60,000. It was refused. The next day, the offer was raised to $130,000, and Rick thought that was enough. They settled.

Later, exiting the courthouse, they were asked by a juror what the settlement amount was, as the jury had no idea what to award, should they get the case. It seems the juror thought, as Sylvia did, that they could have gotten much more money.

After expenses and legal fees, Rick netted $90,000.00. When he got the money, he started donating to all of the TV evangelists he had been watching. The 700 Club was one, but perhaps the largest was Jimmy Swaggart. Later, Swaggart's infidelity scandal would devastate Sylvia, but by then, Rick had passed away and was spared the disappointment.

Of course, they also donated to their church, Glad Tidings. Their pastor was interested in building a new church and moving out of the old theater. They found a parcel of land off of Route 1 in Malden, high on a hill. With the land purchased, the church was built with funds procured via inventive loans. The members would lend money to the church at two points higher than the going bank rates, and could get their money back when it was needed. Rick and Sylvia started at $30,000.00, but the amount was raised to $50,000.00.

With the settlement money in hand, they no longer needed assistance from the State. Having had only enough money to buy really old cars, they splurged on a four-year-old Lincoln Continental, perhaps the best car they ever owned. They ate better, too, eating in restaurants most of the time. They had a few niceties, but not many.

One last effort was made to help Rick with his battle with cancer. Doctors convinced him to take chemotherapy. While Sylvia was against it, Rick sided with the meager 5 percent chance of making it.

At this point, they became volunteer counselors for the 700 Club in Malden. They saw many miracles there, and they enjoyed their work, finding it very rewarding. But Sylvia could see Rick failing fast. There would be no miracle for him.

It was now the summer of 1986. Watching television from his bed, Rick called Sylvia to join him watching Jerry Falwell. Falwell spoke at length about abortion and how many babies were aborted each year. Falwell, explained that he ran a home for homeless pregnant women so that they could get help and shelter and, most importantly, keep their babies. He said he had put together a manual called the "Save-A-¬Baby Syllabus." It was a manual to instruct anyone interested in starting a shelter similar to the one he had in Lynchburg, Virginia. If anyone were interested, he would gladly send the manual, free of charge, to instruct him or her, step by step, on just how to fund and set up a shelter. Instantly, Sylvia felt God was telling her to get the manual. She told Rick that this was what she wanted to do, and ordered the manual, she still has it to this day.

Still counselors for the 700 Club, Rick and Sylvia's manager encouraged speaking in tongues. It was thought that speaking in tongues was communicating in heaven's language, if one considered what was spoken not to be gibberish but understood that person was filled with the Holy Spirit. Coming from a Catholic background, Sylvia shied away from this notion. That is, until she had a dream.

She dreamt she was taken up to heaven. She saw Jesus there. She saw a round table at which several men sat. She didn't count them but it seemed to her there were twelve or more. They talked to each other and then they all prayed in tongues over her. Sylvia, in this dream, also started speaking in tongues. It was her baptism of the Holy Spirit.

Thus renewed, Sylvia prayed for confirmation from God that (as far as the home for unwed mothers was concerned), if this was really what He wanted her to do. She received that confirmation in another dream.

She was holding the infant Jesus in her arms and he was dressed in royal garb, much like the famous Catholic statue "The Holy Infant of Prague." The infant began to speak to her, but in the voice of an adult male. He said the wedding garment is all prepared and she was going to prepare the flowers for the wedding. She took this to mean that Jesus was describing children who would be born at her home and those already born who would come with their homeless mothers. In the Bible, Jesus sometimes referred to children as "flowers."

Because she used to literally prepare flowers for weddings, she figured He used the term meaning that now it would be His "children" for His "wedding." Sylvia, as a result, was convinced she was on the right path.

Although Rick was just six months from his journey home with the Lord, he worked diligently to assist Sylvia in getting the shelter started. He found a Christian lawyer, who drew up the articles of incorporation. He followed through with the incorporation with the State of Massachusetts, pro bono, with what Sylvia and Rick chose for a name, at the time it was "New Life".

They got a letter from the State, stating "New Life" was not acceptable. They asked Sylvia and Rick to contact them. Sylvia called an official, from a public phone booth. She was informed that "New Life" was a very over used name and they requested she change the name, Right then, she blurted out, "Life for the Little

Ones." She had never thought of or heard the name before and she was sure it came from God, and was to become a true ministry. The lawyer also started the process of getting the non-profit status with the federal government.

On January 25, 1987, Life for the Little Ones (LLO), Inc. was itself born. Rick began networking among other Christian pro-life groups, introducing him and Sylvia, explaining what they planned to do. One of these groups was Pregnancy Help, a referral agency. It was a Catholic outreach group that would talk to desperate pregnant women and offer them a solution to their dilemma. Pregnancy Help would contact shelters that were willing to house and help them through their time of need. One such shelter was Friends of the Unborn. Rick and Sylvia visited and spoke at length with the owner. They were also given copies of the rules and regulations followed by Friends of the Unborn and the occupants of the homes. These would prove invaluable in the future.

On March 27, 1987, Rick was at home and became paralyzed from the chest down. He lay across the bed, and Sylvia had a hard time repositioning her 200-pound husband. However, after much ado, she successfully had him back at the head of the bed in a vertical position. For the rest of the night, he confessed his sins to her as though she were a priest. He told her that he had loved her from the moment he first laid eyes on her. He said, "God gave me a ten-foot angel and I didn't even know it." Sylvia replied, "I'm no ten-foot angel, I'm five foot Sylvia."

Rick knew it was time to go to the hospital. Rick told Sylvia that he wanted her to call for an ambulance to take him to the hospital the following morning. The next day, after she called the ambulance, she tried to dress Rick but couldn't he was so heavy. The ambulance came with two big men. She explained that she had tried to dress him to no avail and would they please dress him for her. They tried unsuccessfully. One attendant asked Sylvia if she would allow them to roll Rick in one of her bed sheets onto the stretcher. Sylvia gave her consent and Rick was put in the ambulance.

She stayed with Rick all day Saturday. On Sunday afternoon, while Sylvia's family was there, and with the complete absence of Rick's alienated family, Rick looked at Sylvia's children and said, "You are my family." Her family left at about 5:00 PM. Sylvia lingered behind for a few minutes to say goodbye privately. At that point, as she was about to leave, Rick asked her to place the nurse-call button in his hand. She did so and went home.

She went to bed about 9:00, exhausted from worry. At about 9:15, she got a call from Rick's nurse. He could not reach the phone, and had her place the call. She handed Rick the phone. Rick said, "I'm going to die tonight. Would you come to the hospital?" There was an urgency in his voice.

She left home as quickly as she could and arrived at 9:40 PM. She had him repeat the Sinner's Prayer after her one last time. Comforting him as lovingly as possible, she told him, "You are now a child of God, and God is with you." At this point Rick said "Go get the girls." And I'll always take care of you." Then Rick picked up on what Sylvia said, and kept repeating over and over again "God is with me," with every breath he took, they were heavy, deep, and slow breaths.

Even though all of the paperwork was in place, Sylvia had not actively started looking for pregnant women to help. For the past two months, she had her hands full with Rick. To this day, Sylvia knows he continues to protect her.

At about midnight, the doctor and two nurses came in. They said, "Mrs. Anthony, you should go home, you need the rest." She felt that they were the ones who wanted to go home. Rick was still repeating, "God is with me. God is with me." His eyes were beginning to roll to the back of his head. She called his name at about 12:20 AM, but got no reaction. The repetition continued. She was getting concerned about the late hour, and a fear gripped her about going into the poorly lit parking garage alone. She decided to leave before it got any later. But truthfully, she could not bear to see him take his last breath.

At about 5:00 AM, she received the call from Rick's doctor. He had just gotten in and found Rick dead. Rick went home with the Lord on Monday, March 30, 1987. He had completed his task and laid the foundation for their ministry.

For two days, Sylvia felt twinges of guilt that she had not stayed until the very end. However, during the night of the second day, she felt God was telling her not to fret, Rick died right after she left. God had spared her any additional pain. She felt a bit better. She knew God had taken Rick home. Before he died on that Monday, he was as pure a soul as a person could be. He was completely spiritual. Sylvia felt full of the Holy Spirit. People would remark at her appearance. She felt they could feel the presence of the Holy Spirit in her. To her, it was truly a blessed experience, as though she had received an award straight from heaven. There were no tears to mark Rick's death then—just a holy peace.

During all of this ordeal,, even though the foundation had been laid for "Life for the Little Ones, Sylvia had not actively started looking for the pregnant women in need of her help, she was trying to pull herself together.

One Saturday morning after Rick died, Sylvia phoned her daughter just to chat and to see how she and her family were getting along. Her daughter was in her bedroom on the second floor. As they were talking, Sylvia heard a male voice—Tony's voice—call out to Lynda from the living room on the first floor. He asked, "Lynda, is that your mother?' Lynda shouted that it was. Tony was on his regular Saturday weekly visit that Sylvia knew nothing about. He replied, "Tell her I'm sorry Rick died." Sylvia said, "Tell him thank you." At this point, Sylvia really was not in the mood to talk to him.

Chapter 13

For about a month, Sylvia had what she called her "pity party." She then took hold of herself and started to look up the people she and Rick had gone to see. She went to Pregnancy Help and spoke with the woman they had talked to before. Sylvia was ready to house some women. Not long after, she got a call from her contact. It seems there was a girl who was living in jail at times simply to get off the streets. Her mother had thrown her out of their house when she was only fifteen. She was also pregnant.

On May 5, 1987, Sylvia picked up her first girl. Theresa was seventeen years of age and of Italian descent. So it was that Sylvia took Theresa home to her rented apartment in Everett, Massachusetts. It was the second floor of a two-family house. Sylvia would take this girl everywhere she wanted to go.

Theresa was seeing a man at the time, a musician, and she took Theresa to see him wherever he was appearing. Things seemed to be going quite well at that point, but she noticed Theresa was very reluctant to help with the housework, and never wanted to do the dishes. Sylvia was new at this and made concessions she should never have made.

Running her new operation at her own expense, Sylvia needed some help. At first, she requested one-third of the girl's income from welfare. Theresa tried very hard to avoid this, and frequently got away with it. Sylvia then applied to Operation Blessing for some assistance. The manager of the 700 Club was very helpful. He would ask her how much she needed, but she would always take just a little. She could have gotten much more than she requested. Not long after, two other girls joined Sylvia. She now had three pregnant girls living with her 24/7.

It was May of 1987. Sylvia's daughter, Lynda, was pregnant with her second son. On the evening of May 28, Lynda visited Sylvia rather late at night, about 11:00. Sylvia was surprised to see her so late. Lynda explained that she was in labor and asked Sylvia to take care of her son so that she and her husband could go to the hospital together. She gladly agreed. As her daughter was leaving, she asked Sylvia if she would call Tony when the baby was delivered. Sylvia was surprised at this request, but she agreed.

Sylvia took her grandson and put him to bed. The following morning, after she and her grandson got dressed and had breakfast, Sylvia proceeded to go about her busy day as scheduled. She took her grandson with her wherever she went, doing so by public transportation because her car was having a new motor installed. Her grandson was enjoying this thoroughly. He had never ridden on a train before. As she went from appointment to appointment, she would check with the hospital approximately every two hours to ask if her daughter had delivered her baby.

At approximately noon, she called the hospital and they said she had not delivered yet. At 2:00 PM, she called and they said Lynda had delivered her son at noon and everything was fine. At this point, she recalled her daughter's instructions to let Tony know when the baby was born. Coincidently, this was Tony's fifty-eighth birthday. When she called Tony, he answered and she simply wished him a happy birthday and told him of Lynda's baby's birth. Tony replied, "Is that you?" To Sylvia, this was a foolish question, who else would call and tell him her daughter had her baby. He then requested she meet him at the hospital.

Sylvia then took her grandson back home, fully intending to go to the hospital right away. When she arrived at her house, she found Lynda's husband waiting for her. He was sitting in his car in the driveway. She was very surprised to see him and asked him if everything was all right. Much to her surprise, the story she got from him was totally different from the story she got from the hospital.

He told her that Lynda was in intensive care, and that the doctors had to operate at the last minute in order to save both mother and child. Sylvia then said she was on the way to the hospital, and asked if he would please take her. He was exhausted, having been up all night, and had nothing to eat all day. With that, Sylvia instructed her son-in-law to take the three of them to a local pancake house. She could do nothing to replenish his lost sleep, but certainly could aid in caring for the body.

After they ate, Sylvia suggested they all go to the hospital. She told her son-in-law that she called Tony, as instructed, and he would be waiting for them. He agreed to take her, but cautioned her on what to expect. He said he was the only one allowed to see Lynda.

When they arrived at the hospital, Sylvia's grandson said, "There's Tony." Sylvia replied, "Where?" He pointed in Tony's direction and said, "Over there." He had been waiting at the hospital for four hours for them to arrive. Sylvia felt very uneasy; after all, she hadn't seen Tony in seventeen and a half years. When Tony approached her, the conversation immediately turned to the problem of the day. He spoke to her as though they had never parted. He said he had tried to see Lynda, but was not allowed. At this point, Sylvia's son-in-law spoke to Tony. He asked Tony to take Sylvia home. He explained that he was very tired, and said that he not only wanted to but desperately needed to go home and rest. Tony replied, "My car is old." As though he was ashamed to have Sylvia see his old car. However, Sylvia's son-in-law insisted, stating the age of the car didn't matter. Sylvia agreed. Tony conceded.

Tony took Sylvia to his car. Along the way home, he stopped for a cup of coffee so that they could talk awhile. The first thing he said was, "Thank you for all the years of pleasure you gave me." Sylvia was a bit embarrassed. Especially, since now she was a new creation and her old ways were gone.

She was wearing her wedding band and Rick's ring that she had adjusted to fit her finger, plus a gold cross Rick had bought her. He remarked that she was now wearing a lot of jewelry. She just smiled. The rest was just general conversation. He then took her home. Lynda recovered in a few days and was released from the hospital.

Lynda began inviting Sylvia to her house on Saturdays. She spent the time with her family and Tony. The days were very enjoyable, and in the evening, her son-in-law would prepare a gourmet meal. Following dinner, they would watch a movie together until ll:00 PM. There was only one thing she would have changed if she could: the choice of movie that the son-in-law Paul and Tony liked to watch. They were of the very violent type. When Sylvia asked one time why they liked this type of movie, their reasoning was it was not the violence, they liked but the special effects. Sylvia said no more. Men!

After the movie, Sylvia and Tony would leave at the same time. They would chat privately for a few minutes, outside the house, before getting in their cars and Tony would kiss Sylvia goodnight. They would then go their separate ways.

One Saturday afternoon, as Sylvia, Tony, and her daughter were having tea, Tony, surprisingly, reached in his pocket, pulled out his wallet, and began to thumb through the pictures it contained. He pulled out one in particular. He handed it to Sylvia and asked, "Do you remember this?" It was a pin-up picture of Sylvia when she was 21 years of age.

Sylvia at 21

He had kept this picture in his wallet for thirty-seven years. It was a bit frayed around the edges, but very much intact and well preserved. He must have taken it out of his wallet to look at many times.

Sylvia's daughter became curious and asked to see it. No one but Sylvia and Tony knew it existed. When Lynda saw her mother in the very seductive pose, she was quite surprised. But what was more surprising was that Tony had kept it all these years.

After about four of these Saturday gatherings, after Sylvia and Tony left the house, before they each got into their own cars to go their separate ways, Tony pulled Sylvia aside. He said that he would like to get back together and pick up where they left off. Their relationship seventeen and a half years ago was a commitment that was complete in every way. They saw each other each day, cared for the children, and enjoyed time together. They had gone for long rides to the beaches, movies, and many other places. It also included a physical relationship.

Sylvia had become a born-again Christian and her views on sex without marriage were totally different now. No way was she going to agree to "taking up where they left off," in the physical sense. When he asked to do so, she snapped her head and looked at him with glaring eyes. They had known each other for so long and never really had to speak very much; they could sense what the other was thinking. When Tony saw her reaction, he knew this time things were going to be different.

Sylvia and Tony began a new relationship, but it was a totally different one. Also, now that Sylvia had become a Christian, she had totally forgiven him for past mistakes. She no longer harbored any resentment. They began a relationship with a clean slate, one based on pure love and respect for one another. They, in reality, became soul partners. They resumed going on pleasure rides together. At times, when they went on a new route, as they often did, Tony would question Sylvia as to which way to go. Sylvia would tell him to go straight, thinking that, eventually, they would come to a familiar intersection. Tony found this to be a perfect opportunity for a pun. He said, All my life, you have been telling me to go straight." This became a standard joke with them.

One day at Tony's house, his sister Gingy, asked him to take her somewhere. Well, it was not so much a request as a demand. Finally, at the age of fifty-eight, Tony refused her. The sister was furious, how dare he refuse her. Tony turned to his sister-in-law and begged her to explain to Gingy, that he had a right to a life of his own.

Chapter 14

Before Rick went home to the Lord, he saw an announcement on TV about a trip to Israel. He told Sylvia he would like to take the trip and walk where Jesus walked. He had her send in the deposit for the trip. This was very strange, because he had a dreadful fear of flying. The only trips the pair made were by car in the U.S. Knowing how ill he was, he told her to make the trip, even if he couldn't. The trip was scheduled for August 30, 1987. Of course, Rick didn't make it. He was with the Lord permanently.

One week before the trip, Sylvia's landlady told her the girls had to go. The apartment was rented to Sylvia and Rick. There were no provisions for the extra women, and she wanted them out before Sylvia left for Israel. Sylvia was frantic, and quickly began looking for a place for the women. She couldn't believe her landlady, who also became her friend, could be so merciless.

Three days before she was to leave on the trip, she found a house to rent in Stoneham. The owner was an electrician who had just purchased the property, and was in the process of doing some electrical work. He assured Sylvia that the work would be done by the time she got back from her trip. It wasn't! The owner lived next door and agreed to watch over the women. On hindsight, Sylvia's old landlady had really done her a favor. How could she possibly expand or go on with these women in the old apartment?

During this time, Sylvia received a call from an agency and was told of a pregnant woman who would be coming in from Boston's South Station by train. She had nowhere else to turn. They asked if she would take her. Sylvia agreed. They told her she was a graduate of the Julliard School of Music and a professional violinist. She would be recognizable not only because she was pregnant, but she would also be carrying a violin case with her luggage. However, all the time she was at the shelter, she never once played it.

Soon after Sylvia returned from her vacation, she quickly looked for another location. In the local paper, she located another house that was for rent in Everett. It was only three years old. She called the owner and made an appointment to see the house. When she met with the owner, she explained that she had a home for homeless women and was interested in renting her home for them. The owner explained that the only way she would rent the house was if Sylvia lived there too. Sylvia felt this would not be a wise move, but she was so impressed with the house, she said she would rent it for herself. She gave the owner a deposit and the move was set for November 1, 1987.

That evening, when Tony arrived, she informed him she was moving to another house in Everett and suggested they take a ride by so that he would know how to get to it when she moved. When Tony saw the impressive house, he asked the cost. She told him that the rent would be $950.00 per month. Tony was shocked when he heard the cost. Keep in mind, Tony lived at home with his parents. The home they owned was completely paid for, and what he paid his parents for room and board was very minimal. To him the cost was prohibitive. Tony asked, "Do you realize that is nearly a thousand dollars a month?" Sylvia replied, "Don't worry, God will provide." After all He always has.

She was so happy with her new home, she would play audiotapes of praise songs to the Lord and sing along with them every day. When Tony would let himself into the house after dinner, he would find Sylvia singing. One time, he said, "When I come in here, I feel like I'm walking into a church." She would continue living there for nine and a half years.

After Sylvia moved into her new home, she continued looking for a home for the girls. She found a condo for rent in the City of Revere and quickly vacated the premises where the girls were living. They needed to move because of the landlord's neglect in completing the renovations he was required to make. Tony would help her on occasion, but still thought it all to be a bit strange.

One way he really helped was when she was on vacation. She would take a vacation during the winter months to escape the cold. Tony would always take her to the airport, no matter what time it was and would faithfully pick her up when she returned and take her home. While she was away, he went to her house daily as though she were there. When it snowed he would shovel the snow. One time while she was away, it snowed three times. Three times Tony shoveled the snow. When she arrived at the airport, there were mounds of Massachusetts snow piled everywhere. Tony, picked her up and took her home. To her great surprise and thankfulness, the sidewalk and entrance to the house were completely shoveled. Tony enjoyed being the unofficial caretaker of her property when she was gone. That was just Tony!

As Sylvia was looking after the needs of these women, she began to realize the great need there was for her services. There were a vast number of women that were out there that needed help. She knew that she needed a much larger facility, one that could house 100 women and their children, at a time. She thought this was her idea, but God had a plan for her and her ministry that would not be realized until sometime later.

While she was getting organized in her new home, unpacking boxes, she found the letter she had gotten from Robert Schuller's advertising agency,(Douglas Lawson Advertising Agency} with those interesting questions. Since she now had a board of directors and the 501©3 non-profit status the agency had inquired about, she wrote them again, including all that had been accomplished to date. About a week later, she received a call from a secretary, inviting her to New York City to attend an all-day seminar for non-profits. The seminar cost $100.00, but Sylvia was invited to attend at no cost. She needed only to get herself there and home, and she could bring someone with her.

Sylvia chose a very loyal volunteer to accompany her. Vera was all excited when told of the pending trip and insisted on paying her own way. The seminar was most interesting. They learned a lot of the potential pitfalls of such organizations and ways of working around them. During the morning break, she had an opportunity to approach her sponsor and introduce herself. She reminded him of their correspondence, and told him of her desire to have a complex that would help 100 girls. He invited her to tell her story to the audience, and she jumped at the chance.

A Catholic nun heard Sylvia speak, and asked if she would join her for lunch. During the conversation, the nun told her that the Archdiocese of Massachusetts might be willing to donate one of their empty homes, but this never came to fruition.

At the end of the seminar, another woman approached. She said she was running a home for homeless boys in Brooklyn, New York, and that H.I.M. Ministries had drawn up the plans for the home built with grants and donations. She gave Sylvia a name, David Sammey, and his address. He was the man in charge of H.I.M. in Brooklyn. Sylvia wrote him as soon as she got home.

Mr. Sammey, in turn, contacted the president of Helps International Ministries in Harlem, Georgia. The president sent his son to Brooklyn, and he and Mr. Sammey drove to Sylvia's home in Everett to meet her. Sylvia made them lunch and told them of her dreams. She wanted a chapel, an administration building, a daycare facility, a school, and enough housing for 100 girls. After lunch, Sylvia took them on a tour of the area and pointed out the types of buildings she envisioned would suit her desires, including a small chapel and other buildings. The son went back to Harlem Georgia with the notes and wishes Sylvia had described, and the architect drew up a plot plan and sent it to Sylvia. All the work was done free of charge.

Sylvia began sending out proposals to corporations requesting financial help in the form of grants. Since her proposal included that the shelter was an alternative to abortion, a very political topic, most of the companies refused—except a few. All of the hard work done by H.I.M. was relegated to a file drawer, but only for a few years.

Chapter 15

The relationship with Tony became a closer one. Every evening, after it was evident they would not be going out again, Sylvia would excuse herself and dress in her evening clothes to relax. When it came time for Tony to leave, he would escort her into the bedroom. She would jump into bed and Tony would hug and kiss her good night and tuck her in.

The condo in Revere now had five women and two babies, in residence. As time went on, two of the women were ready to move on, they had found section 8 housing. One woman moved to Beverly the other Winthrop, the towns they originally came from. They had graduated with honor. Three new arrivals came. One had a miscarriage and went back to her boyfriend. Then Sylvia received a call from an agency, telling her of a young girl who was arriving. Her baby had been born prematurely, and the baby was still in the hospital.

Soon the condo seemed too small, a much larger place was needed. She found an old mansion on Ocean Avenue in Lynn, near the Swampscott line, one block from the ocean, it had four large bedrooms. One of board members assisted in moving the women from Revere to Lynn.

At this point, Tony began getting totally involved. He worked side-by-side with Sylvia, taking the women shopping, to schools, to appointments with doctors, and to hospitals during the birth of their babies, and for pre-and-post-natal checkups. They also visited the women in the hospitals after the birth of the babies. Clothing donations came quickly. The women had to want for nothing material, and could work on their personal lives.

Because of a lack of funds, Sylvia was taking no salary. As a result, the vehicles she had were all very cheap used cars. Tony fixed them again and again to keep her transportation capabilities up. They would go to the Boston Food Bank, where they purchased food, paper products, laundry supplies, soap, cosmetics, and other necessities, for ten cents a pound. This helped the women tremendously. Tony did most of the lugging of the heavy cases and enjoyed all that he was doing. He said he really felt like he was doing something very worthwhile.

At this point, there were four women living in Lynn. One of the women had her baby, and the other three weren't due for five or six months. All of the women loved the new baby. It was as though the baby had four mothers. The child's mother asked Sylvia if she would take her to Swampscott to apply for a housekeeping job. Tony and Sylvia took her and she left the baby with them outside while she was taking her interview. It was a beautiful, warm day, so Tony took the baby and walked up and down the road with the baby in his arms. Tony truly felt very needed, and enjoyed the baby very much. The baby never cried; she just enjoyed the love she felt. He walked up and down with her, till her mother was through with the interview. Unfortunately, the mother, Kristen, didn't get the job.

One Friday evening, Sylvia received a call from Kristen. She explained that one of her friends from Long Island was coming to see her and would Sylvia mind babysitting for the weekend, as she had never been out socializing for six months, since the baby was born. However, Sylvia was already committed to attending a pro-life march in Washington, D.C. She felt very bad, but had to decline. Kristen's friend left Long Island, and motored to Lynn to see her. It was a snowy winter night, and in mid way, she put up for the night at a motel and continued the next morning. When she arrived Kristen told her she had no one to baby sit. Her friend suggested that they take the baby with them to Long Island for the weekend.

After a long and grueling ride, the threesome arrived at 10:00 PM, with the baby very cranky, hungry, and tired. Kristen could not seem to quiet the baby and, out of anger and frustration, yelled to the baby "I hate you!" It was not the baby she hated but the father who left her when she became pregnant. The baby looked just like him. The memories of abuse fired her feelings for a moment.

The next morning, Kristen realized it was quite bright. She had overslept. That's when she went to the baby and found her blue and unresponsive. Baby Joan was dead. Her death was attributed to sudden infant death syndrome. Kristen was devastated.

When Sylvia returned from the D.C. march around 1:00 AM, she noticed she had a message on her machine. It was from the other girls at the shelter; she heard their panicked pleas for a return call. What dread waited? Making the call, Sylvia could not believe the tale told by the girls of the baby's death. Kristen had called her only friends, telling them the full and awful story.

The only thing Sylvia could do was put her floral design skills to work, creating a floral heart memorial. With two friends, she made the agonizing trip to Long Island for the baby's wake. Crushed, Kristen retreated to the arms of Sylvia and they cried together. Eventually, Kristen returned to Massachusetts only to pick up her belongings and return to Long Island. That was in 1989.

Sylvia had asked Tony if he would like to go with her to the baby's services. Tony refused. He just couldn't face the anguish he would experience if he went to the funeral. He loved the child so dearly, and her death tore him apart. It took three years before he was ever able to pick up a child in his arms and hold it again. Kristen later went back to Long Island, married, and had three more children: a girl (who looked just like her) and two boys.

After having had no contact with Kristen for nearly sixteen years, in February of 2007, Sylvia received the following e-mail:

Hello, Syl – remember me?

You were the angel of my life in 1989, when I needed you most. It is one of the deepest regrets I carry with me that I left Lynn/Marblehead to come back to New York after Joan died. But, I was scared and lost and clinging, once again, to a man I thought would save me. On the other hand, I have three gorgeous kids now. Who am I to regret anything that God has turned into a blessing for me?

Still, I struggle with life as though I was never meant to live it simple … I'm still working on all those things that challenge me, and will never give up or give in.

Across all the time and space that separates us, still I am with you, praying for you, and believe that I remain in your prayers all these years later. I am living in New England now, rebuilding my life from the ashes yet again, and would love to hear from you someday.

Be well, Sylvia, and live as long as Methuselah, for there are many more like me who need your unconditional love and limitless devotion.

Yours always,
Kristen

Chapter 16

One day, Sylvia's son Dan went to visit her at her new home. When he arrived, Tony was there. Dan stayed for quite a while and everyone enjoyed the visit. As Dan was leaving, he invited Tony and Sylvia to his house for dinner. Dan was married now, with one daughter. About a week later, Tony and Sylvia took up on Dan's invitation. They had a very pleasant evening together. During the conversation, again Tony took out his wallet and removed that same picture of Sylvia. He probably felt that now that her children were adults, he would show them what she looked like at age twenty-one and, more importantly, that he loved her enough to carry this picture close to him for all those years.

From this point on, Tony began attending some of the family gatherings. Once, Tony and Sylvia attended a birthday party for Dan's wife. Also attending the party was one of Dan's friends, who had known Dan since their high school days in Brookline. Dan had grown up to be a self-made man. He had put himself through college, obtained a master's degree in business administration from Babson College, and was now a vice president of a large banking institution in Boston.

Dan had told this very close friend how Tony was the only father he ever knew and how much of an important part he played in his life. Dan's friend had heard a lot about Tony, but had never met him before. When Dan's friend approached Sylvia to say hello, Sylvia introduced Tony to him. He must have heard from Dan that Tony was now seeing his mother again; he replied, "So, this is Tony! You're the man who raised Dan. I must tell you, you did a very good job." Tony just smiled and nodded.

Then there was Paulette, yet another client, who was due to deliver the following March. One Sunday in March, after Sylvia returned from church and had her lunch, she received a call from one of her former clients. She said that she had been with Paulette all morning and was trying to reach Sylvia: Paulette was in labor. She had taken it upon herself to take her to the nearest hospital that morning, believing Paulette was going to deliver very soon.

Paulette was supposed to be taken to a hospital in Dorchester. Marie thought there was no time to take her that far away. Paulette was admitted to the closer hospital, but was sent home shortly thereafter because she had dilated to only two centimeters and had a long way to go. When she explained the situation, Sylvia simply instructed Marie to check the frequency of her pains. Marie was told to call her when they were about ten minutes apart.

Tony was due to arrive very shortly, and, sure enough, he did. He asked Sylvia where she wanted to go. He suggested a ride to Rockport for the afternoon. No sooner did he make the suggestion than Sylvia received another call from Marie: Paulette was having pains every four minutes. Sylvia turned to Tony and told him they were going to the girls' house because Paulette was having her baby. This was the first experience Tony ever had actually taking a girl to the hospital while she was in labor.

When they arrived at the house, Sylvia took Paulette aside. Paulette was quite anxious. Sylvia told her, in a hushed manner, to stay calm and not to scream. That would get Tony nervous. He was a bachelor and he had never been in this situation before. (This was all true, and it seemed to help Paulette a bit.)

Paulette, Marie, and Sylvia got in the car, and Tony proceeded to go to Paulette's designated hospital on the south side of Boston. Paulette was trying to be very quiet, but every so often, she would moan with each pain. While in the Sumner Tunnel, one of two underneath Boston Harbor, Paulette began vomiting all over the place. Sylvia kept tossing napkins to Marie in the back of the car to keep cleaning up the mess. What made matters worse was that there was a traffic jam inside the tunnel. Traffic was at a standstill for approximately five minutes. He told Sylvia later that he almost ran out to see if he could find a doctor.

When they arrived at the hospital, the nurse on duty seemed quite annoyed. She said Paulette wasn't ready because Paulette had been calling her all day. But she did say she would have a midwife examine her. When she examined Paulette, the midwife told the nurse that Paulette must be admitted right away. She was then eight centimeters. Sure enough, thirty minutes later, a baby girl was born. Paulette became the longest resident client Sylvia ever had to that point. She stayed with her for one year and ten and a half months.

She and Tony watched these young ladies grow into responsible adults and watched their children grow. Later, Paulette went to school to get her GED. Tony and Sylvia would drive her to school and pick her up. Even after Paulette graduated from the shelter and went into her own apartment in Dorchester, she would call Tony and Sylvia if she was in need of a ride to get groceries or whatever. Sylvia and Tony would go willingly and help whenever needed.

Paulette especially liked lemon meringue pie. Every so often, Tony would purchase one, and he and Sylvia would take it to her. She eventually met a fine young man a minister's son. They married and now have four children.

Chapter 17

Sylvia began having physical problems soon after she and Tony were reunited. She didn't say anything to anyone. Three years later, she could no longer ignore the problem. She was hemorrhaging profusely. The problem was compounded by the fact that she had no medical insurance, and for the past three and a half years, she had no income. She had donated more than $22,000.00 the first two years of the ministry to get it off the ground, and took no salary thereafter. She was living a very minimal existence.

In 1990, a board member, after finding out about Sylvia's illness, recommended she see a female doctor who took care of his mother. He spoke to the doctor about Sylvia's condition, and she suggested that Sylvia call for an appointment. The appointment was made, and after talking to Sylvia awhile, she soon realized Sylvia had no funds to pay for any medical procedure. She then suggested that Sylvia have an interview with the hospital credit department. When she spoke to them, she explained that she had no income and was running a shelter for homeless women. They asked her if she had a board of directors, and she affirmed that she did. They then asked her to bring them the minutes from board meetings for their review.

Although the doctor had stated she would be willing to wait for her money, the hospital saw in the minutes a clause that stated, when possible, Sylvia should be given an annual salary of $30,000.00. The only problem was that at that particular moment, the ministry was only grossing $30,000.00. Therefore, in order to build the ministry, she took no pay.

Sylvia tried to tell them that she would be paid only when and if the funds were available, but they didn't believe her. They refused her admission.

As matters got worse, she prayed to God to show her what to do. As she was praying, she got a revelation to call the New England Baptist Hospital. That morning, she did exactly that. The receptionist answered the phone, and Sylvia explained her problem, both physically and financially, hoping not to waste their time and hers.

The woman was very helpful and said they had a physician referral service at the hospital, and she would immediately try to find one who would be willing to see her. The receptionist said she would call Sylvia back within thirty minutes. This was on the Friday of the first week in June 1990. She was true to her word; exactly one half hour later, she called Sylvia and told her that a Dr. Paul wished to see her on Monday.

When Sylvia went to her appointment, she took some newspaper articles about her ministry to prove she was telling the truth. Dr. Paul examined Sylvia, and exclaimed, "You have cancer of the uterus." He then said, "I believe in what you are doing in your ministry, and I want to help. With that, he asked his nurse to go with him to the administration office of the hospital, to see if they would allow him to give her free care. They returned in about ten minutes and had the good news that they could. With that he asked his nurse, "When is the earliest date we have vacant in the operating room?" She replied, "One week from the upcoming Thursday." The doctor was obviously very annoyed with that answer. He gave her a very dissatisfied look. However, he quickly got hold of himself and said nothing more.

On Tuesday of that week, Sylvia went about her daily routine with her women and returned home at 5:05 PM. There was a message on her answering machine and she played it back. It was Dr. Paul's nurse, and she wanted a call back as soon as possible. Sylvia called immediately and the receptionist answered. Sylvia explained that she had received a call from Dr. Paul's nurse, and was returning her call. She said that Dr. Paul's nurse had just left, but she knew why the nurse called. It was to tell her that they would like to have her come in for pre-operative testing the next morning. It seemed another operation, which had been set for that Thursday, had been canceled. Dr. Paul wanted to schedule Sylvia's operation to replace the cancellation. Sylvia was sure Dr. Paul arranged the change, although no one said so.

Wednesday morning, Sylvia went for the tests and was admitted Thursday. At that point in time, Sylvia was attending the Wellesley Baptist Church. The pastor of the church went to the hospital to visit Sylvia before the operation and prayed with her. Later on, the pastor and his wife visited Sylvia at the hospital on three more occasions, and they finally met Tony.

The operation was a success, but for some reason, Sylvia wasn't recovering as she should. Dr. Paul ordered a CAT scan and instructed the nurse on what to do. Sylvia was kept heavily sedated. Tony visited Sylvia every single day, even though he had a phobia against heights; she was on the sixth floor and he never would go near the window.

During the evening following the CAT scan, she prayed to God.

"Lord, I don't know if You want me to continue in this ministry. Whatever You wish, Thy will be done. If You wish to take me home, that's fine with me; it's better up there than it is down here."

That evening, while she was asleep, she had a vision. As she was lying on her bed and looking at the ceiling, she saw the face of Jesus looking down on her above the right corner of the bed. A great light appeared like a spotlight. It started out small at the ceiling and got larger and larger as it descended. The beam covered her whole bed. His face showed only for a few seconds and disappeared, but His voice remained. He said, "I am sending you down sheets of protection." Then she saw sheets that looked like four-by-eight panels coming down from the ceiling.

Like the spotlight, they would start out very small and get larger and larger till they were the same size as the bed. They hovered over her bed about a foot apart. They were white and about an inch thick and very sturdy, not floppy. As each sheet came down, Jesus would say,

"This is for your respiratory system, this is for your nervous system, this is for your digestive system, this is for you mental capabilities, this is for your muscular system, this is for your hearing, this is for your sight, this is for your soul."

When she woke up the next morning, she felt completely new, like she had never felt before in her life: no aches, no pains, just perfect. When Dr. Paul and his nurse came in that morning for their usual morning rounds, his nurse looked at her in amazement. Sylvia looked like a new creation, totally healed. She looked at Sylvia and exclaimed, "Well, you're among the living." Sylvia smiled and nodded agreeably. She was as amazed as the nurse. Dr. Paul then told her that she could go home in two days. The power of God has no limits. At this printing, that incident was nearly twenty one years ago. Sylvia is now 81 years of age and never has the cancer reoccurred.

Sylvia's sister Lydia went to the hospital to visit her every few days. When she heard the good news, she invited Sylvia to stay at her home for a month, so that she could look after her. She prepared breakfast and dinner for Sylvia, but had to go to work during the day.

Tony would go to visit Sylvia at about 11:00 AM each day and take Sylvia out for a ride and to lunch. He would return her to her sister's house by mid-afternoon and leave. Then he would return in the early evening and watch television with Sylvia and Lydia.

As Sylvia began to feel better, she felt as though she was imposing on her sister. Tony was coming every day, anyway, so that after a week and a half, she told her sister that she no longer needed to stay at her house. Sylvia moved back home. However, Sylvia was very grateful for the time she did stay with her sister, and never forgot how caring she was throughout the ordeal.

Tony continued to look in on Sylvia every day and would spend much more time with her. He took her out every day and made sure she ate properly. Sylvia fully recovered. God's intervention was very clear. Tony became an even more loyal companion, asking for nothing and doing whatever had to be done in the ministry, whenever needed.

He was also beginning to get very interested in becoming a Christian. He told Sylvia that she had something he wanted, a seemingly boundless inner peace. Sylvia never pushed her religious beliefs on Tony. She knew he would have to make his own decisions. After he left Sylvia in the evening and returned home, he would put on the TV and watch evangelists. On his own, he made a commitment to become a Christian.

From then on, he assisted Sylvia every month to prepare Communion on the first Saturday, for the service the following Sunday. He also assisted Sylvia in decorating the church with fall decorations for Thanksgiving, and would hang wreaths and set up candles for the Christmas services. Everything he did for the church was without fanfare. Most of the church members didn't even know how the church got decorated.

On very rare occasions, he would attend a Sunday service or a church gathering. The first time he attended a service, the pastor left the altar and walked all the way to the back of the church where Tony was sitting, just so he could shake Tony's hand and welcomed him.

On another occasion, Tony accompanied Sylvia to a service. It was a practice at the church, for anyone who felt like making a request for prayer, or wanted to pray aloud could do so spontaneously. At this point, Sylvia began praying aloud, praising God for all He had done for her, physically and in her ministry. She also asked for blessings for all the members of the church. After she completed her prayer, Tony spoke out, loudly, and said, "Ditto." With that, the pastor spoke out and said, "Tony, that's the first word I ever heard you speak in this church." The whole assembly laughed.

Sylvia was in desperate need of a car. There was no more repairing the one she had, and Tony convinced a man he knew to donate his car to Sylvia. Once a year, beginning in 1987, Sylvia would plan a solo trip for a well-deserved rest. Tony never wanted her to go, but never complained. He realized she needed the break, and stayed behind. He would go to her house while she was away and look in on the women at the shelter and do whatever needed to be done.

It was also around this time that Sylvia met a woman who was interested in becoming active in the ministry. Loretta and her husband Peter had two teenagers from a previous marriage and a three-year-old daughter of their own. She became a member of the board not long after, and introduced her husband to Tony and Sylvia. They became very good friends, and every two months, they would meet at Loretta's home to work on the bi-monthly newsletter, titled, "Sylvia's Haven News."

During the two days that it took to compile and address the newsletters, Sylvia and Tony would order pizza for the group. It became a very enjoyable time of fellowship and work. This friendship is still intact, and Peter remains as treasurer of Sylvia's Haven, Inc., volunteering his time without any fanfare for more than twenty two years.

Chapter 18

Cathy's Story – 1992

Born in Casablanca, Cathy came to the United States in 1987. Cathy was a very bright woman, who spoke five languages fluently. But because she was new to this country, she could get a job only as a live-in nanny. She would take the baby for strolls in a nearby park each day, where she eventually met a man and a relationship developed.

She desperately wanted to stay in the country. She allowed herself to get pregnant by the man. Her plan was to force a marriage that would let her stay. When she told him she was pregnant, however, and he in turn told his mother, the mother would in no way allow a marriage.

As it became obvious that she was pregnant, her employers confronted her and asked that she confirm their beliefs. Cathy could not and did not deny anything. They told her that they would pay for an abortion or she would have to leave, as she was a poor example to their children.

Cathy wanted the baby badly. Knowing she had to leave the nanny job, she quickly sought shelter. She found it with another organization run by a woman named Rosemary.

Over the course of several months, Rosemary saw in Cathy several very strong traits that made her a resident manager. But Cathy also had an "Old World" nature about her and would come on strong at times. That was a turn-off to some people— including Rosemary.

Sylvia and Rosemary knew each other for some time, and Sylvia would get a call from her anytime she wanted to pawn off one of her problem clients. Such was the case with Cathy.

In the fall of 1991, Sylvia decided to take her in. She was thirty-nine years of age and pregnant. When Sylvia and Tony went to pick her up, she had two large leaf bags full of clothing. The two were surprised that she had so much.

Cathy worked out well for Sylvia and was again made a resident manager. Sylvia tolerated her strong managerial style because she always kept the other women very much in line.

When it came time for the baby to come into the world, Sylvia took her to the hospital. It had been decided that Cathy would have to have a cesarean section. Sylvia was there for the whole procedure. It was the first time she had witnessed a C-section; she was awed by the procedure.

As time went on, Cathy moved into her own apartment, but always chose one that would keep her close to Sylvia. She visited Sylvia regularly and would even attend family gatherings. They began a relationship that eventually would soar a few years in the future.

In September of 1991, Sylvia's father got into an automobile accident. A young man went through a red light into her father's path. The car frightened him and instead of hitting the brake, he hit the gas, and charged into a telephone pole. His head hit the windshield and left a bubbled imprint. Being eighty-one, he had heart problems and was taking Coumadin, a blood thinner. He was rushed to the hospital. His brain was bleeding and the doctors could do nothing about it. They sent him a priest but he rejected the offered help.

Later, when Sylvia and her father were alone in his room, she asked him if she could come back and pray for him. Although he agreed, she never did pray for him; Somehow something deep inside kept her from going. A failure she regretted for years. She continued to visit him, along with her mother and sister. Two days before his death she heard him cry out, "Oh God, oh God, oh God," it was his way of asking for forgiveness. Sylvia is certain he had made his peace with God.

Years later, Sylvia told a group of women of her regret not having gone back to the hospital to pray for him. One woman spoke up, telling Sylvia he had to make his peace on his own. Looking back she realized the woman was right, and decided that God had held her back.

Her father remained in the hospital for about a week. He died on September 18, 1991. It was at that point that Sylvia got rid of all the resentment she had held toward him and forgave him completely. She realized his philandering was the result of an addiction that he could never overcome. She was sorry his life ended the way it had, but was glad he had finally called on God, and was sorry for his sins. She is sure God forgave him.

Chapter 19

For ten years, Sylvia had rented whole houses with a minimum of four bed-rooms. During those years, God assisted eighty-seven women and seventy-three children under Sylvia's roofs.

In May of 1992, Sylvia received a letter from the federal government informing her that Fort Devens, a Massachusetts-based army camp, was withdrawing from 48 percent of its occupied property. The letter stated that because she had a shelter for homeless women, she was eligible to apply for housing on the base through the McKinney Act, which stipulated all bases which were closing should reserve a section of the facility for the homeless.

The available property was also listed and gave the name of a Mr. Bill Sumner as the contact person. He was an army major charged with the task of overseeing the dismantling of the base at Devens. The letter concluded that she should contact Major Sumner, if she was interested.

Interested? Sylvia was so excited that she immediately called Tony and told him about the letter. They both felt this was a fantastic opportunity. The letter stated that the cost of her lease would be $1.00 per year, and the deadline for proposal submission was July 1, 1992.

Next, Sylvia called her lawyer, who had been working pro bono for her for more than a year. She told him of the letter and read it word for word to him. Without hesitation, he said, "Let's go for it." Sylvia met with Mr. Sumner and chose fifty townhouses and a chapel.

The letter of intent was written, and her lawyer began to write the proposal. Sylvia did all the legwork necessary to give the lawyer all the information that was needed. The lawyer worked very hard, and the full proposal was completed and sent overnight the night before it was due.

The thing that drew Sylvia to this was the fact that it was going to cost all of a dollar a year. She thought God really did have a sense of humor. She supposed that if He could rope her in for a dollar a year, He would then take care of the rest.

The proposal was reviewed for her board of directors. It included how the fifty townhouses and the chapel building would be used. Descriptions of where house-mothers, a maintenance person, and a supervisor would live there were included as well.

A portion of the chapel building (which was a 22,250-square foot structure) would be set aside to house the president/executive director of LLO. A full day care center, clinical rooms, offices, teaching rooms, and storage units were also included.

It was also at this time that her board voted to include not only pregnant women but also battered women, their children, and homeless women who are not pregnant. If the proposals were accepted, room for all of that would not be an issue.

Thirty days later, Sylvia was notified that the proposal had been accepted. Soon after the approval, Sylvia was told that the four towns bordering Fort Devens had formed what they called a, "Housing Alliance." This group met once a month. The towns involved were Ayer, Lancaster, Shirley, and Harvard. Now that Sylvia was a member of the community, she was invited to attend their monthly meetings.

During all this, Major Bill Sumner was the official overseeing the downsizing of the base. The federal government formed Fort Devens in 1917 on about 5,000 acres of land. Initially, they leased, and then later purchased, the land from 112 owners holding 230 parcels in the 4 towns. Now that the army was leaving 48 percent of the base, the land was to revert back to each town. Each town had the original boundaries of their town, and each was to get their piece of the pie back. They formed their housing alliance to determine what they would do with this newly re-acquired land.

During all this, Major Bill Sumner was the official at Devens overseeing this process. But in August 1992, Sylvia got a call from one Rhett Donelly. He wanted to meet with her and give her a short tour. He seemed friendly, gave her a tour of a three-bedroom unit, and offered her an office on the base. Although the base would be officially closed until October 1995, she might be able to move into an office on an interim basis.

She declined because she could see no sense in having an office there three years prior to actually moving in, since she was located thirty-seven miles southeast of Fort Devens. She was living north of Boston, near where her clients lived, so she would be available to help in any way they might need—and no one needed her help more than Lena.

Chapter 20

❧

Lena's Story – 1993

Unfortunately, not all client stories are ones of success. Having always had a 95 percent success rate, at times, the heartbreak over the remaining 5 percent was almost too hard to bear. Sometimes, personal or family problems stemmed from birth, and Sylvia could do little to help. Lena's case was one such heartache.

She entered LLO in March 1993, while Sylvia was still in Everett. On the first meeting with a client they are given an application to fill out and a copy of the rules they are required to follow. One of the rules is that the client, if she had a history of an addiction to drugs or alcohol, must be clean for at least one year, and this must be verified by a doctor or counselor. Lena never mentioned that she had such a history. She was accepted, but Sylvia could tell however, that she seemed disturbed.

On June 4, 1993, Sylvia received a call from another client, Kathleen. Lena had a seizure. An ambulance was called and she was taken to a local hospital in Everett. Kathleen was with Lena during the seizure and went to the hospital to try to help. Lena was admitted and was undergoing tests of all sorts when Tony and Sylvia arrived to see how she was.

The medical staff said Lena had what was called a grand mal seizure. There are many causes of this epileptic paralysis, but several of the most common are congenital defects (which are present from before birth), injuries that occur near the time of birth, the use of alcohol or other recreational drugs, or withdrawal from alcohol or drugs. Beating or other trauma to the brain could not be ruled out either. Since she had been admitted, there was nothing else for the group to do but go home. On the way, Kathleen told Tony and Sylvia about Lena's family, just as Lena had told her.

Lena's divorced father was the head doctor at a north shore hospital, and her mother a head nurse at another institution. The mother was a morphine addict. The behavior continued into her pregnacy with Lena, and Lena was born addicted to the drug. The father abused Lena, psychologically and sexually.

When Lena called her mother from the hospital, her outreach was met with the cold, could-not-care-less statement that she would be all right and to just call her back the next day. Sylvia prayed for Lena at the hospital several times. Her client notes quote: "Praise God, Thank You, Jesus, for curing her." After a few days, Lena was discharged.

On July 22, 1993, a little more than a month and a half after her first admission, Lena called Sylvia on a phone, stating she was lying beside a dumpster all night long, and now made it home and would she please come and take her to the hospital. Lena had been beaten, had her Walkman stolen, and was suffering from bumps on her head, a few nicks, a bitten finger, and some broken ribs. When Sylvia arrived to provide the transportation, the other women at the house told her they thought Lena was back on drugs. Not yet convinced, Sylvia took her to a clinic in nearby Lynn.

After a checkup and dismissal from the clinic, Sylvia took her home. On the way she cashed a $100.00 check Lena's father had given her. Lena was not seen at the shelter again until late the next day, when she called Sylvia. She said she had a lapse of memory and had blacked out. This was not true—as Sylvia soon discovered by Lena's own admission.

The women at the shelter had seen some rather strange behavior from Lena for about two weeks prior to being taken to the clinic. All were concerned but didn't know the cause. Lena finally told Sylvia that her father had once again raped her. This was the cause of all of the turmoil. He obviously had been doing so for years.

Ever cautious about the stories told to her by her charges, Sylvia contacted Lena's psychiatrist and, with more than a bit of effort, confirmed her story was true. When asked why the psychiatrist had not brought in the authorities, she said that Lena had refused to testify on the stand for obvious, ever-present fear. Sylvia suggested that Lena testify on tape. Ignoring the suggestion, the therapist simply said she would look for another hospital that could care for Lena. It came out later that the therapist had been retained by Lena's father.

A week after being admitted to a hospital in Belmont on July 26, 1993, she was granted a one-day furlough that she spent with Kathleen. After another week, Lena went back to the shelter, but within days, was caught smoking crack cocaine by others at the shelter. Sylvia had no choice but to remove Lena from the shelter. Lena left on her own, taking very few of her things with her, only those things she thought she could sell. She was seen later at a local variety store, trying to sell a radio. However, she still cared for and was greatful for Sylvia's attempted help. Lena called Sylvia a day later and asked if she could be driven to her mother's home. Sylvia, having given up on the presence of Lena in her shelter, had not quite given up on Lena herself.

On the way to the mother's house, they talked extensively, and the fact that Lena had been born an addict came out. Sylvia became so angry, she couldn't wait to confront the mother and give her a large dose of her Sicilian rage. Lena told her that her mother would not answer the door. Her habit was to get her dose of morphine, when she was leaving work, go home, lock the doors, disconnect the phone, and go to bed.

Sure enough, at the house, Sylvia rang the doorbell, and rang it and rang it. All that was left for Sylvia to do was leave Lena on the front porch with all of her belongings. She dreaded doing so, now knowing the long and frightful history of this poor young woman. Sylvia prayed to God for His help in protecting Lena. Sylvia had done all she could. The pain was great, nearly overwhelming, and the sadness and feeling of failure remains to this day. Several attempts at finding her have failed.

Chapter 21

Sylvia's dream for her shelter on the Devens property continued with some modifications. Despite the Devens tour of the three-bedroom townhouse with Mr. Donelly, she later found out that there were two-bedroom units also, and the amount of space available for her clients was cut dramatically. She submitted a revision to her proposal that included more units, a tennis court, and an officer's club located nearby. The revised proposal was turned down.

About two months after approval of her first proposal, Sylvia was having a tough time getting to sleep. As was her habit, instead of lying restlessly in bed, she got up to do some work until she got tired enough to finally sleep.

She started looking for some important papers she had to review. She came across the old plans drawn up by Helps International Ministries several years ago. When she looked at those plans, something odd struck her. She quickly grabbed the Devens plans and compared them. She was amazed at the similarity. The two sets of plans, drawn years apart, were almost identical. She sat in awe for two or three hours, and realized they weren't her plans at all—but God's all the time.

As for the monthly meetings held by the four-town alliance, Sylvia and Tony attended them all. They also attended a meeting with officials from Washington, D.C. (connected with the army) to discuss plans for her entry into Fort Devens. Poor Tony was overwhelmed. When he was in the army, he was a private and was made to look up to his superiors. The presence of these officials, now on par with him, was an awesome experience for him.

About a year and a half into those meetings, there was talk of yet another meeting to be held, now between the town alliance and The Redevelopment Agency, (TRA) a quasi-state agency. They proposed that the towns turn the property over to the Agency, which they would turn it into a commerce center, putting all the people who were hurting back to work.

TRA began holding meetings with the citizens of the four towns involved in the breaking up of the base. Over a period of one and a half years, there were six such meetings, during which the Agency made glowing projections and presentations on the redevelopment of the base parcels. To the four towns, they hoped, it would be most enticing and help gain local voter support.

When Sylvia chose fifty base townhouses and the post chapel, she had no idea of how the property lined up; she just was impressed that she got what she had chosen. On a tour of one of the units, before the proposal was written, she was impressed with the spacious, three-bedroom home.

It turned out that she had picked property on Harvard soil, making it the most valuable of all. After the end of the sixth meeting, a special election of all four towns, was held in Harvard, to vote on whether they were willing to give up their claims to the parcels of land being vacated by the army.

Lancaster voted to turn its portion over because theirs was a marshy wildlife reservation. Since it was the only town of the four that was rather affluent, Harvard opted to retain its portion of the land. The other two towns sorely needed the increased revenue the redevelopment would bring in, and opted to give their property to the TRA.

Now that the TRA owned the land, the TRA would become her landlord, when a lease was signed. Sylvia was told she would have a lease with the TRA as soon as they took over in the spring of 1995. The Agency clearly saw that Sylvia had twenty and a half acres of the very best location in the town of Harvard. However, because the Federal Government had approved Sylvia three years before, the TRA takeover would not affect her.

It must be repeated here that Sylvia had been given fifty townhouse units 50% were two bedroom units, and 50% were three bedroom units, on twenty and a half acres of land, in strips. Most had eight units side by side. One had four and one had six.

The units were individual two story townhouses and each family had their own townhouse. The post chapel was a grand 22,250-square-foot building. It not only had a chapel, but also twenty-two additional rooms, which Sylvia intended to use for all kinds of purposes. Her personal residence was included. The building sat on a hill on five acres of beautifully landscaped land, and included picnic tables, benches, and a state of the art playground for the children living at Sylvia's Haven.

It took twenty-seven months for both parties to agree to the terms of a lease that both could abide by. This grueling task was very disheartening to Sylvia. Finally, her lawyer suggested she sign the lease offered by the TRA, to at least get a foot in the door. Life for the Little Ones, became Sylvia's Haven, Inc., in April of 1994. Her board felt the name should be changed in order to attract corporations. The abortion issue was too political.

Henceforth, Sylvia's Haven would now be open to all homeless women, regardless of their situation. The move into Devens was initially scheduled for three years in the future, the amount of time it would take for the Army to vacate the premises. However, it took nearly five years before the lease was signed.

Chapter 22

Sylvia realized the vast quantity of clothing, food, and furnishings she was going to need for fifty houses full of mothers and their children, and started preparing for this major move. Five years before the actual move in date, she appeared occasionally on radio and TV nationally on The 700 Club. She went to places where large numbers of people were gathering, passing out literature, speaking at churches, and speaking to anyone who would listen. She made it known that she would accept clothing and furniture from anyone who wished to help. Soon, clothing and furniture donations were coming from everywhere.

Sylvia was still living in the second Everett house. It was a split-entrance ranch with a one-car garage. She occupied all of the upper level and approximately half of the lower level. The other half had been made into an in-law apartment that was also rented out.

As the donations came in, Tony would assemble shelves and racks along the wall of the garage, family room, and office to organize the donations. As time went on, the car could no longer fit in the garage. There were donations from floor to ceiling and front to back. Soon, people began calling for pick-ups. Tony willingly went whenever there was a need.

One time, a single woman in her mid-twenties heard of Life for the Little Ones. She began purchasing about $50.00 worth of goods each week, and stored the goods in her small three-room apartment. She bought umbrella strollers, bedding for cribs, stuffed toys, and a myriad of children's things. Just before Christmas, she called Sylvia and told her she had some things for the women, and asked if someone could please pick them up. She implied they were taking up too much room.

Tony and Sylvia went to her apartment, and much to their surprise, there were umbrella strollers lined up against the wall of the hall. In the kitchen, in front of the cabinets, and on the floor of the living room were all kinds of goods. They were thoroughly amazed. The following year, this same woman began accumulating goods once again. This time, she decided to purchase comforters. She said she wanted the girls to have something new when they moved to Fort Devens.

Again, just before Christmas, she called implying that her apartment was overloaded again. When Sylvia and Tony arrived, there were comforters everywhere, on top of counters in the kitchen as high as the ceiling, even over the stove, (she obviously ate out), and on the floor, leaving only a path to walk through. They filled up Tony's car, but one car full was not sufficient to transport all she had. For the next trip, Tony suggested Sylvia should take her car also, there were so many of them. The two of them went back for the second trip.

The donor lived on the second floor of the apartment building, and luckily had an elevator. Tony and Sylvia would fill the elevator to capacity, leaving room only for their bodies. They then would bring them down to the lobby and throw them on the floor, (they were in individual plastic zippered bags). They would then bring the cars to the entrance and proceed to fill each the car.

While the comforters were lying on the floor covering the lobby, a tenant in the building was entering. He asked Tony if he really needed all of the comforters. Tony simply said yes and continued packing the two vehicles. Suddenly, a policeman arrived on the scene and asked Tony where he had gotten all the comforters. He explained that the woman on the second floor was donating them to a homeless shelter. They went up to her apartment to confirm Tony's story and left. The comforters numbered 200. Now with all of these extra goods, Sylvia had to give up her family room for storage as well.

The Lexington Christian Academy heard of what Sylvia was doing and offered, as a community service, to bring a classroom of children to her home in Everett to help sort and pack goods. They came during the Easter season each year. Sylvia and Tony would order pizza and soda and give a pizza party after they completed the tasks.

It soon became evident that they would have to rent some storage space. They searched for a space, and found one and rented it. Tony alone would take the goods from Sylvia's house to the storage bin. Sylvia would help, but Tony wouldn't allow her to carry very much. In reality, he did about 80 percent of the work. Never did he complain, and never did he ask for anything in return. He would say that he enjoyed it. It gave him a real feeling of worth.

About a week later, one of the members of the church Sylvia was attending spoke to her after the service. He explained that he owned a motel and was changing all of the furniture, including box springs and mattresses. He told her he wished to donate them to her ministry. Sylvia quickly agreed and had a meeting with her board of directors, to inform them of what had transpired. She also had the problem of where the furniture was to be stored. She went to see Bill Sumner, the officer in charge of the base breakdown, and asked if she could use some of the empty houses for storage. He was very nice and gave her permission to do so, he turned over the keys to the units she could use.

A few of the members offered to help move the goods from the motel to the Devens property. It took two days, and Tony again did about 60 percent of the work himself. The furniture was very heavy, and it filled the first floors of three townhouses.

Then one day, an acquaintance Sylvia knew through some church connections came to her house. Sylvia related her exasperation with the fullness of the house. She didn't know what she was going to do. She couldn't fit much more there and couldn't afford the cost of any more rental space. He told her of a pastor he knew who was given a warehouse as a tax write-off.

The owners had been trying to sell it for seven years and finally decided to give it to the pastor who had been renting the second floor of the building, using it as his church. He said he had an appointment with the pastor later that day and would see if he would be willing to give up a portion of the warehouse for her use.

In a few days, Sylvia received a call from the pastor, and they made an appointment to meet. Sylvia took some literature with her, and after he heard about what God was doing in this ministry, he made his decision. He thought God wanted him to use the warehouse, but now he knew He wanted it for Sylvia. He offered her as much space as she needed, free of charge, for as long as she needed it. God provided everything.

Not long after, a woman called Sylvia and said she heard of a pastor in New Hampshire who was given new cribs and youth beds by a manufacturer—approximately 200 of them. She gave her the name of the pastor and his phone number. When Sylvia called him, she told him she heard he had the furnishings and asked him if he would be willing to donate some of them to her ministry. He was a very good man, was very interested in what she was doing, and asked her many questions about her ministry. Then he asked her how many she needed. She said about fifty youth beds and cribs together, but she needed mostly cribs. He told her he would gladly give her whatever she wanted, but that she would have to send someone to get them. He had no means of transporting them.

Again, Sylvia called a board meeting and informed them of the opportunity to get new cribs and youth beds. One board member said she knew a man who rented U-Hauls. She thought he would let them have one at no cost. Then another member said he knew of a church member who wasn't working who would be able to pick them up. This time, Tony had only to help unload the U-Haul when it arrived. They were put in the garage temporarily. Within six months, the warehouse was nearly full.

Some members of the church of the people who owned the warehouse, decided to throw a benefit concert, the proceeds of which would go to Sylvia's shelter. There was a woman who had attended the concert. She had a son who was a Boy Scout and wanted to become an Eagle Scout. The woman called Sylvia and explained that she bought two tickets, she thought, to another concert, but instead bought the tickets to Sylvia's Haven's benefit in error.

Sylvia was asked to speak at the benefit and let the audience know of her work. The woman said she felt it was God who led her to this concert instead, and what a good opportunity it would be for his Eagle Scout project to do something for Sylvia's ministry. Sylvia was very pleased.

The woman's son decided he would like to completely furnish one house. He worked hard with his parents and friends, and got the project completed mostly with donated goods. With cash, he purchased things that completed the project. He rented a storage room until it would be time to move into Devens and his family paid for it.

It was also about this time that Cathy (the former client who had given birth by cesarean Sylvia witnessed) came to visit Sylvia. She had been living only three blocks from Sylvia. Her little boy, now about five, had been leading the way to Sylvia's since he was two.

On this visit, however, Cathy said she had moved to Malden, quite some distance from Sylvia. It was a change from her usual preference of staying close. Sylvia thought it rather odd, but said nothing. Cathy was, of course, a grown woman and could do as she pleased.

Cathy invited Sylvia to her new apartment. When Cathy had started housekeeping on her own, she had furnished her apartment with yard sale and flea market items. Because of that, even though she was particular about how she chose, her furnishings rarely matched. Now, however, all that was gone, replaced by furniture that did match. It seems she had married, and the furniture was her husband's.

Cathy went to a drawer and took out her marriage license, showing it to Sylvia. Astonished, Sylvia read the name of the groom: It was her son, Teddie Junior. Cathy had been attending many gatherings with Sylvia's family and met Teddie and started dating. Teddie was a forty-five-year-old bachelor.

At one point, Teddie had told his mother that he was thinking about getting married, but he never mentioned Cathy's name. He only said that he had a girlfriend and she had a little boy. He asked Sylvia what she thought, explaining that most available women his age had been married, divorced, and had a child or two.

Sylvia suggested he consider finding a much younger woman, to start his own family. That he took as disapproval, and never mentioned the subject again. If he had said it was Cathy he wanted to marry, Sylvia would have approved. They quietly got married anyway in the Everett City Hall by none other than the mayor. Now one of Sylvia's clients had become her daughter-in-law.

Chapter 23

In the spring of 1997, she knew the lease for the Devens' property would be signed in May, and she began looking for a house to rent in the Devens' area. Concentrating in the towns of Groton and Harvard, she finally found one in West Groton. A split-entry house, it was rather small, but she moved in on May first and made it work. Rent for the house was $1,000.00. Her board had long since approved reimbursing her housing costs, and approved the slight increase from what she was paying in Everett.

Shortly after moving in, her lawyer suggested that she sign the lease with the Redevelopment Agency. He said, "You would at least, have your foot in the door." She signed in May of 1997. The expenses to run the new operation were exorbitant. The insurance alone required a million-dollar umbrella policy. The premium cost about $3,000.00, not counting a first-time charge of more than $12,000.00.

Sylvia had to bring all of the buildings, including the chapel, up to the TRA code, keep in mind these buildings had been lived in and were all up to the army's standards. They insisted she add new wiring, and new plumbing. She was to remove all of the windows on the second floor of each unit and replace them with large picture windows. They wanted more lead paint and asbestos removed than required, and insisted she install new sprinkler systems throughout the whole complex.

When she questioned the need for a new sprinkler system, she asked, "Why must I put in all new sprinklers, there is no law in this state that mandates sprinkler systems must be installed in residential homes?" Their reply was, "We know, but our insurance premiums would be lower."

As soon as the lease was signed, the insurance adjuster was to come down to inspect all of the property, including the chapel. Sylvia and her insurance agent inspected the property first to be sure everything would be approved.

When they were given the chapel, however, the ceiling was badly in need of repair. It was a real mess. There were buckets strewn throughout the building to catch the water leaking from the ceiling. The roof had to be repaired in order to save the chapel from mass deterioration. The boiler was almost inoperable.

When the insurance broker inspected the building for possible coverage, and saw all of the buckets, he told Sylvia she would have to have the roof fixed before the insurance company would even consider coverage.

Lacking the funds for a new roof, something had to be done fast, to get the building insured. She hired a roofer to patch it, and finally, the chapel was insured. The incident was a rude awakening for Sylvia. All of the renovations and repairs were going to cost an enormous amount of money.

She decided to divide the work into five phases, four of which would deal with the fifty residential units and the fifth would deal with the chapel. It was more important to get the residences for her clients first.

Every year since they acquired the property, work had to done to repair the boiler. It was so huge (1 million BTUs) that they couldn't afford a direct replacement. This expense could not be ignored or all the pipes would burst and there would be no chapel.

Once the Devens lease was signed, the problem was to transfer all of the goods from the different storage areas to any available space in the townhouses. It took thirty-two truckloads of furniture and goods to empty the various storage locations. Tony moved 85 percent of the furnishings himself. At this point, he was sixty-eight years of age.

Work began on phase one of the renovations that included two strips of townhouses, one with eight units and one with six.

Sylvia, in her rented Groton house, converted her living room into a temporary office. But she soon found out that the quick decision she had made on her rental was a big mistake. Her house had been rented before to a lieutenant at Fort Devens. That lieutenant had a dog. The dog had fleas. Many had been left behind. The rugs were infested with them.

She also came to know some animals that many city dwellers didn't. Chipmunks, what many call "chippies." She was fascinated with them. One evening, she decided to prepare a meal for them. She took some bread, and broke it into little pieces and put it in a large paper container, and left it on the kitchen counter, intending to toss the bread in the yard in the morning.

When she got up, she found the cup on its side empty, and lots of mouse droppings over the counter Not slightly irritated, she left the mess as she found it. She was to meet with her landlord later that day,

He arrived about 11:00 A.M. She quickly took him to the countertop, and showed him the evidence of a rat infestated house as well as fleas. She told him she had flea bites all over her body. However, he was a very arrogant man, admitted that he knew of the rodent problem, and simply suggested she put out some traps.

That was the last straw for Sylvia, she immediately began looking for yet another home. She was not going to stay in that house a minute longer than she had to. She contacted nearly all of the real estate brokers in the area.

She found a very nice executive-type house in Groton. She thought, with all the moving to Devens, what was one more move, under the circumstances? The rent, however, escalated to $2,000 a month. A member of her board, living in a less opulent house, drove the issue, and she was not granted anything at all for rent.

Tony found it difficult now to do as much as he had before. The distance between Boston and Devens was thirty-seven miles. He did, however, still go to the Boston Food Bank with Sylvia about two or three times a month to get food, paper products, laundry products, cleaning products, toiletries, personal care items, and cosmetics for the women in the complex.

Other than those days, he would visit Sylvia every day, in the evenings. He would leave his home after dinner each night at 5:15 PM. He didn't reach Sylvia's house until 6:50 PM, because of rush-hour traffic. When he arrived, they would either go for a ride, weather permitting, or stay home and watch TV.

Tony would leave precisely at 10:00 PM. Before he left, Sylvia would change into her nightclothes, as was her custom, and relax as they watched TV. When it was time for Tony to leave, Tony would go upstairs with Sylvia to her bedroom, tuck her in bed, and sit at the edge of her bed a few minutes before kissing her good night.

At Devens, Sylvia now had a full crew working for her— one resident manager for every three units, a groundskeeper, and an office assistant. (There will be more about the work being done later, as it impacted Sylvia's Haven greatly.)

As time went on, the board felt that Tony and Sylvia shouldn't have to be the ones to go to the food bank for supplies. But Tony enjoyed doing it, so they continued in this manner. After a while, Tony began to realize that he wasn't getting any younger and going to the food bank meant that he had to do a lot of heavy lifting. He finally agreed it was time to stop this run, and Sylvia appointed two employees to go to the food bank when needed.

By this time, Sylvia was able to have more than one vacation a year, perhaps two or three, lasting from five to twelve days. Tony never went with her, but never stopped her from going. There was a time, however, when he asked her if the trips could be limited to one week. This was difficult, since the cruises and tours she took had set schedules to adhere to. He understood, but missed Sylvia terribly. While she was gone, he would maintain his routine as if she was home. He had a set of keys to her house and would go and watch TV all alone, then leave at the same time he would if she was home.

On the weekend, Tony would go to Sylvia's house at about 2:00 or 3:00 PM and stay until his normal departure time in the evening. They would still go for their rides, at times, and on the weekend, they would go out to dinner. When they were seated at a restaurant, Tony never sat at the opposite side of the table facing Sylvia, but sat next to her, to be as close as possible. When watching the television they each had their own couch. There was always a sense of togetherness that was comforting. Sylvia felt secure just to have him there.

Sylvia was soon confronted with yet another tragedy. Her mother, now eighty-seven years of age began suffering from dementia. Since she lived alone, Sylvia's sister, Lydia, would look in on her in the morning before going to work, again during her lunch hour (she worked close by) and again when she got out of work.

One morning, Lydia could not get in her mother's house. The door was locked from the inside. When she looked through the pane of glass in the door she could see her mother lying on the floor outside of the bathroom door and she could not get up. Lydia went next door for help, the home of a fireman. He called the fire department for help. By this time her mother had forgotten how to cook and there was a fear, if she attempted to make a meal, she might get burned. When the firemen arrived, they had to force the door open. They picked her up and sat her down. Lydia now had to make a quick choice as to what to do next. She had no choice but to have her sent to a rest home where she could be properly taken care of.

All during Sylvia's eighteen and a half years at home, she would sense a cold-ness from her mother. She had not abused Sylvia, as her father did, but she never showed any outward affection toward Sylvia. When she went into the rest home, however, she must have felt sorry she hadn't shown her daughter any love. Now, every day, when Sylvia visited her, she would get all excited. She would hug and kiss her continuously for about a minute before letting her go. Sylvia and Lydia were surprised at this new behavior from their mother.

Sylvia did not realize the extent of her mother's dementia until one day when Lydia and Sylvia visited. Their mother was chilly and Lydia went to get an extra blanket. Her mother turned to Sylvia and asked, "Where did that girl go?" Sylvia did not know what girl she was talking about. Sylvia asked, "What girl?" Her mother replied, "That girl that was just here. Where did she go?" It was at that point that she realized her mother really didn't know either of her own daughters. They were simply constant visitors whose names were not known. It was heartbreaking for the two daughters.

On another occasion, Sylvia, visiting alone, found her mother's room empty. She was worried and began frantically looking for her. An attendant had put her mother in a wheel chair and took her out to the reception desk so the staff could keep an eye on her. When Sylvia headed toward the lounge, where she thought her mother might be, she passed by the reception desk. She saw a patient in a wheel chair with her back facing Sylvia and thought nothing of it. As she got further down the corridor, she went passed the woman in the wheel chair. She heard a voice calling, "You who! I'm here. You who! I'm here". Suddenly, Sylvia turned around to see who was calling. Sure enough it was her mother. But Sylvia was shocked. Her mother now required a wheel chair. It upset her greatly.

As time went on, her mother contacted pneumonia. She was 89 years of age when God called her home on February 11, 1998. Lydia saw to the emptying of the house of furnishings and the painting of the interior, to prepare it for selling. Sylvia acted as the real estate broker during the transaction saving any commissions from being paid.

It was a small 4 room cape, what little they were able to get they divided. Sylvia used this money to help pay the rent on her new home in Groton. Again, God provided. There was one major purchase she allowed herself. It was a baby grand piano for her house, for her Tony, to play whenever he visited.

Every evening after watching TV or playing cards together, Tony would go to the baby grand piano Sylvia had bought for him, and play beautiful contemporary music and love songs adapted from the works of classical composers. Sylvia would sit beside him on the piano bench. He normally would play anywhere between fifteen minutes to an hour, depending on the time and how he felt. The love songs he played were for Sylvia. What he couldn't express in his words, he expressed in his music. It was as though the music was coming right from his heart. These were precious moments for Sylvia. Inevitably, every night, he would include their song, "Till the End of Time."

On Christmas Eve 1998, Sylvia went shopping for food for Christmas Day. Each Christmas and Mother's Day, Sylvia would invite her children and their families for the holiday. She returned just before Tony was scheduled to arrive, and she began to put all of the food away. When Tony arrived, he began picking and eating some of the food she had put away. Sylvia was lying on the couch in the living room watching TV, and didn't think anything of it; this was a routine performed every evening.

While they were watching TV, Tony would get up in the middle of a show, and go into the kitchen to see what he could snack on. Sylvia had no problem with this. As far as she was concerned, her house was Tony's house too.

This time, however, was different. Tony went to the bathroom because he was having a hard time digesting the baked beans he had eaten. He tried to induce vomiting by sticking his fingers down his throat, but nothing came up. It was the end of the night and he was anxious to get home. He told Sylvia he didn't feel well. Suddenly, he started losing his voice, as though laryngitis was setting in. His voice was down to a whisper. He had paralyzed his vocal cords.

When he got home, he told his brothers he was sick and asked them to take him to the VA Hospital. Tony told them to call Sylvia and let her know what had happened. At about 10:00 A.M. the next morning, They called her, to let her know Tony was in the hospital. As soon as she could leave the office, she went directly to the hospital. When she arrived, the doctors told her he had two cardiac arrests during the night and was resuscitated each time. They informed her that the hospital had a lodge for the families of the patients, free of charge. Sylvia intended to stay as long as possible, so she went to the desk and a room was reserved for her. Sylvia was allowed to stay at the hospital free of charge for as long as it was necessary for her to do so.

She stayed with Tony for quite a while that evening. She asked to see the doctor so that he could let her know what they intended to do. The doctor informed her that they had taken a CAT scan. They found not only that he had a heart attack, but also had stones in his bladder and an enlarged prostate.

After speaking to the doctor, she went to her room. She left instructions that, if she was needed, they were to call her immediately. The following morning, Sylvia got dressed to go see Tony. She wanted to talk to the doctors again to find out their intentions.

When she got to Tony's room, he wasn't there. She asked a nurse where he was, and was told that Tony was having another cardiac arrest and they were working on him. The nurse directed her to the room he was in. As Sylvia approached the room, his nurse said, "We were trying to reach you, he's having another cardiac arrest. We're taking him to the operating room."

As they were wheeling him out of the room, Sylvia walked with the staff. Although his eyes were closed, The nurse said "Speak to him, he can hear you." Sylvia said, "Tony, I'm here." He nodded his head to let her know he knew.

After they took Tony to the operating room, Sylvia asked the nurse how long she thought the operation would take. The nurse indicated it could take several hours. With that, Sylvia went to work for a few hours and returned to the hospital. When she arrived, the doctor still hadn't completed the operation. He was performing a quintuple bypass. They didn't even ask permission from the family; there just wasn't any time.

When the doctor completed the operation, he spoke to Sylvia. He told her the operation was a success. He said, "I have done my part, he will be good for another ten years. Now it is up to the others to do their part." He was referring to the stones in the bladder and the enlarged prostate.

About two days after the operation, while Sylvia was with Tony, his brother George, came to see him. When he came into the room, he looked at Sylvia with surprise. It had been approximately fifty years since they last saw each other.

All of a sudden, Tony spontaneously decided it was true confession time and he blurted out, in a few minutes, his whole relationship with Sylvia. He told him they had been seeing each other, how she now ran a home for homeless women and children, and how their relationship was now a purely platonic one. He told his brother how he had helped Sylvia in her work and, seemingly most important, emphasizing more than once that there was no hanky panky going on.

He emphasized it repeatedly, because he did not want his brother or the rest of the family to disrespect her. Often, in the past, when Sylvia would show her dissatisfaction and let it be known she was very upset over the fact that he kept his family from knowing of their relationship, he would reply, quite anxiously, "I'm protecting you, if I told them they would never believe that nothing was going on."

He would say this with such anguish, always afraid that if Sylvia got angry enough, she would leave him again. All of the arrogance he had as a youth was gone. Many times, to reassure her, he would say, "You are the best thing that ever happened to me in my life." When his brothers, and his sister-in-law Mel would visit him, and he talked about Sylvia, he would repeat the same thing to them often.

For the duration of the time Tony was in the hospital, Sylvia stayed in the hospital lodge. After about a week or so, they sent him home, but the hospital doctor told him he would have to return in a week or so, for the operations to correct the other two problems.

After he got home to East Boston, he was in no condition to travel the thirty-seven miles to visit Sylvia. He told her he wanted her to go to his house and visit each evening. This was very strange to Sylvia. She hadn't stepped foot in his house in fifty-five years. However, she did as he asked and visited with him every night after work. At first when he was too ill to move, she just stayed there until about 10:00 PM.

Sick as Tony was, he realized that after working all day and commuting for an hour or more each night to visit with him, Sylvia must have been extremely tired. He would feel so bad, he would get out of his bed and sit on a chair and tell her to lie down on his bed for a while. Sylvia was embarrassed, but she would do as he asked. As she thought about it, there she was lying in his bed taking a nap, and he would just sit by the bed very quietly, and just watch her sleeping or resting content to just have her there.

When it was time for her to leave, rather than go all the way home so late at night, she would stay at a motel close by and leave right from the motel for work each morning. In the meantime, Tony postponed the operation. The thought of another operation, with possible complications and perhaps a long recovery, bothered him.

The overnight stays at motels were hurting Sylvia financially. Tony realized this; sometimes, he would give her the money for the room. As Tony got better, he decided to take his car and go for a ride. It was about 11:00 AM, and because of his medication, he fell asleep at the wheel. The car crossed the street onto the sidewalk and hit the staging in front of the house. But, God was again with him and the staging stopped the car and nobody was hurt, including Tony. This incident was necessary in a way. Now Tony realized he would be unable to drive for a while.

He was very worried that because of the accident, his license might be taken away from him. Sylvia assured him that they wouldn't take his license away for sleeping at the wheel, and he realized she was right.

Tony would want to go on long rides in the evening with Sylvia and she obliged. There was, however, a problem. Sylvia was now leasing a company vehicle, and the contract was for three years at 20,000 miles per year. The long rides she took with Tony and the trips from her work to his house were putting about 1,000 miles a week. She tried to make Tony understand that they should go for shorter rides, but they were his only enjoyment and a way to be close to Sylvia. Sylvia understood and really didn't complain too much. She would figure something out.

He continued to postpone the second operation for three months. He finally realized that he had to have it. The problem was, he was taking aspirin for his heart, and when he went to the hospital to have the operation, they explained that there would be a lot of bleeding with the prostate operation. When asked about the last time he took aspirin, he told them it had been two days. This was much too soon to operate, but they went ahead anyway.

After the operation, he bled so profusely that they had to pump nine gallons of water into his system for fear of blood clots, and gave him three blood transfusions.

Again, Sylvia stayed at the hospital through the whole ordeal. Physically, Tony was never the same again. To walk any distance became a real problem. Although he forced himself to walk and he never complained.

Sylvia could see it was a slow downhill process. He continued to drive every night to Sylvia's house no matter how bad he felt. He began retaining large amounts of fluid. His whole body was swollen. That summer, because of his condition, she decided to forgo any vacation that took her far away from him. She decided instead to take a local vacation in Rockport, Massachusetts. She told Tony she wanted to stay close by, and suggested it could be a vacation that they could spend together.

He could come to see her each day at about 11:00 AM, have lunch and dinner together, go for long sightseeing rides, and in the evening, as always, he could go home. She said she would hire a rental car for this purpose so they could ride as much as they wanted without restriction.

Tony was very pleased with the arrangement, but because of his physical condition, he really didn't feel he could endure eleven hours without rest. However, he didn't explain this to Sylvia, because he didn't want to alarm her. Sylvia, not realizing this, just thought he did not want to be away from home so long. So the plan was altered so he would arrive at the bed and breakfast where she was staying at approximately 4:00 PM, in time to go out to dinner.

Each day when he arrived, they would go out and ride further north along the coast to Rye, New Hampshire. The scenery was very beautiful along the coast. There they found a restaurant that featured baked stuffed lobster. Every night for the nine days Sylvia was at Rockport, their dinner was baked stuffed lobster.

After dinner, they would take another scenic route along the coast for a while, and head back to the bed and breakfast before dark. There, they would watch TV and play cards until it was time for Tony to go home.

Chapter 24

As time went on, Tony became increasingly worse. His legs swelled to at least four times their normal size. His stomach was also swollen, and he found it very difficult to climb stairs. He would have to throw his legs, one at a time, over each step, because he could not bend his legs freely. Yet, he still never missed a day without seeing Sylvia.

She never knew when to expect his arrival because he left East Boston after dinner, at 5:15 PM at the height of rush-hour traffic. What would ordinarily take about an hour, at that time of day, would take a minimum of one hour and thirty-five minutes before he arrived at Sylvia's house. Sylvia would lie on the couch in the living room and wait for him.

Sylvia could hear his car arrive at her driveway and the sound of the garage door as he opened it with his electronic key. She could hear the garage door roll up. She noted that the length of time for him to reach the top of the flight of stairs and enter her kitchen was taking more and more time. She sensed that he did not want to be embarrassed by being questioned as to why it took him so long to get upstairs, so she quietly waited. Once he entered the kitchen area, he would be thoroughly exhausted. He would put his head against the wall and just lean there for as long as it would take to get his breath back.

Sylvia never went to the stairway to observe the nearly impossible task Tony had to get into the house. She sensed he wanted to be left alone until he was ready to go into the living room and be with her. They could no longer go out for long rides; climbing the stairs more than once would have been too much for him. They stayed home and watched TV, or he would play his piano with Sylvia sitting next to him. Some nights, they played cards.

At the end of the evening, he could no longer climb the stairs to Sylvia's bedroom to tuck her in bed for their precious moments together. It got so that the more ill he became, the closer he wanted to be to Sylvia. Normally, when Tony arrived, he would lie down on one couch and Sylvia on another and watch TV. But as time went on, to be even seven feet away from Sylvia was too much.

Tony set up a chair next to the sofa actually touching it where Sylvia's head rested. Once he sat down, Sylvia would lay her hand on his lap just so he could feel her touch. That was good enough for him. He just sat there all night long, probably very uncomfortable, just so he could be as close as he possibly could be.

He also became very sensitive. If something he did bothered Sylvia and she showed any sign of objection, he would be extremely hurt. Sylvia realized this and tried very hard to be very tolerant.

Then one evening, on March 1, 2000, Sylvia had a trip scheduled and wanted to purchase some last-minute things after work for her trip. She planned her time so she would be back at her house by the time Tony got there. However, she got delayed in rush-hour traffic, and arrived home twenty minutes later than she had planned.

When she arrived, she let herself in through the garage, as Tony would. When she got to the stairway, she noticed some blood on the carpet in front of the first step, then more on the second step, and at the landing, where the stairway turns, there was a cardboard box. Evidently, Tony was hemorrhaging profusely. The box contained about a quart of his blood.

Sylvia became frantic and ran upstairs, calling him. She ran to the bathroom and looked through the door toward the sink. She didn't see him. She was running around calling him. Finally, she heard a knocking sound. Since he had paralyzed his vocal cords, he couldn't talk above a whisper and would knock to get attention.

The knocking was coming from the same bathroom Sylvia looked into before. She didn't see him because she looked at opposite end of the bathroom where the sink was, he was sitting on the commode on the other end. There was a pool of blood on the floor, and it seemed like about a gallon of blood in the commode. He got up and walked into the kitchen and sat on a chair. His pants were bathed in blood. The chair was a white vinyl upholstered chair that had now turned red. He put both elbows on the table and buried his head in his hands, and said, "I'm going to die."

Sylvia wanted to call 911, but Tony said he would just rest for a minute and go home on his own. Sylvia knew enough not to argue with him; she kept quiet for the moment. Then she thought she would push the issue. She told him that she would have to follow him all the way to his house to make sure he got there safely, and then drive home again. Then she paused for a moment and asked, "What are you going to do home? What can your brothers do for you? What can I do for you? We're not doctors." Tony relented and asked her to call 911. She quickly called.

At first, the police came to see what the problem was. When they saw the seriousness of his condition, they ordered the ambulance. When the ambulance arrived, she told them to take him to the VA Hospital, because this is where they had all of his medical record. They agreed, until they took his vital signs. Then they refused to take him there because this was a medical emergency, and the trip to the VA hospital was a total of 35 miles. They explained he had to be taken to the closest available hospital. Sylvia called his brothers from her house as they were leaving. Sylvia told them what had happened and that he was being taken to a local hospital.

All of the personnel, police, EMTS and later the hospital staff kept assuming that Tony lived with her. She repeated over and over again that he did not live with her, and that he was only visiting. After they arrived at the hospital, Sylvia presented his driver's license as part of the check-in, when they saw his address, they finally believed that he did not live with Sylvia.

The nurse, at the desk, asked Sylvia if she was aware that Tony was in critical condition. Getting an affirmative response, she then asked if his family knew. She told them she had called them from her house when they were about to leave in the ambulance, to go to the hospital. However, at the time of the call she had not mentioned the severity of his condition. The nurse suggested she call them and let them know immediately.

Sylvia did exactly as the nurse suggested, When she spoke to the older brother, he told her he was not familiar with the area, did not know where the hospital was, and after all, did not drive at night any longer. Sylvia offered to go to East Boston, pick them up, bring them to the hospital, and take them back home.

As she was leaving the hospital, the nurse called to her and asked her where she was going. She told the nurse she was leaving to pick up the two brothers. Now, the nurse knew they lived in East Boston and the hospital was in Ayer, a thirty seven mile ride away, She asked Sylvia, "How long will it take to get there." Sylvia replied, "One hour." The nurse realizing she would be gone for two hours, turned to the doctor said, "She is going to pick up his brothers, it is going to take her two hours, will he last that long?" The doctor said he didn't think Tony would last that long.

Nevertheless, Sylvia felt that whichever way this went, his brothers should be there. She arrived at his house, just as she thought. The two brothers were waiting for her and quickly got into the car. While riding back to the hospital, she explained all that had transpired, warning them that the doctor had his doubts that Tony would be alive when they got there.

When they arrived, Tony was still alive. They had diagnosed that Tony had a bleeding ulcer, but because he was in such poor physical condition, they were afraid to operate. They opted to cauterize the ulcer. During the process, they had to give him ten units of blood.

While Tony was in the local hospital, Sylvia would visit him twice a day, once during her lunch hour, and after work, for a much longer stay. Things seemed stable for about three days, and then suddenly, he began hemorrhaging profusely once again. Again, they cauterized the ulcer.

This time, the doctor told Sylvia that Tony was relying 100 percent on life-support systems. It was as if he wanted permission to discontinue administering the life-support system. Sylvia didn't feel, at this time, it was her call to make.

Miraculously, by the grace of God, Tony's vital signs began improving on their own. With this slight improvement, and before matters got worse again, they opted to fly him by helicopter to a large Boston hospital where they felt they had better equipment to deal with this matter.

When Sylvia went to visit him the next evening, the medical staff informed her of the decision to fly him to Boston. The helicopter had already been ordered and was landing as they spoke. Sylvia quickly got into her car and rushed to the hospital in Boston. She actually got to the hospital before the helicopter. She phoned his brothers and informed them of the change.

During his stay at the Boston hospital, he began hemorrhaging once again. Again, they cauterized the ulcer. Each time they cauterized the ulcer, they replaced the blood loss with ten units of blood. Sylvia spoke to the doctor and he told Sylvia that, at one time, the blood used for transfusions wasn't as carefully screened as it was now, and as a result, the liver would get infected. He added that his hospital made certain donated blood was perfect for transfusions. Sylvia didn't realize it then, but he was warning her of upcoming events.

The hospital administration realized there were issues with Tony's case they would rather not get involved in, for fear of a lawsuit. An ambulance was called to take him back to the VA Hospital where he was operated on more than a year ago. When he arrived at the VA Hospital, they placed him in a private room. It was easier for Sylvia to be close to Tony at this hospital, since they allowed her to stay at the lodge again.

Each day, at least one or two of his brothers and his sister-in-law would go to visit him for a short while. His younger brother would go in the evening after dinner and wait for Sylvia to come in from work. Once again, Tony had a hemorrhaging episode. Again, the doctors cauterized the ulcer. The doctor at the VA also had concerns that Tony was too weak to withstand an operation.

Tony's illness at Sylvia's house began on March 1, 2000. Tony had now been in the hospital for nearly a month. He knew Sylvia had a trip scheduled for the end of March. She didn't really want to go, under the circumstances, but she couldn't possibly cancel the trip on such short notice.

Sylvia reminded him of her upcoming trip, and Tony was obviously not pleased with the thought of her leaving him at such a crucial time. He asked her how much she had paid for it, thinking he would give it back to her so she could stay with him. Neither one of them had excessive amounts of money. Sylvia would save in advance for her trips. When told the figure was $5,000, it was evident Tony couldn't match it. That was the end of the conversation.

Sylvia really didn't want to leave, but she didn't want to lose her money. When the time came for her to go on her cruise, she let her office have her itinerary, and instructed her assistant that if anyone in Tony's family wanted to get a hold of her, her assistant was to be sure to let them know how to reach the ship and to reverse the charges. On the ship for only two days, she received a call from her assistant, who told her that Tony's brothers were trying to reach her; Tony had taken a turn for the worse.

When Tony's younger brother called, he explained how Tony got another hemorrhaging attack. This time, the doctors felt they had to operate. There was no other choice. They had to take a chance. Tony could not live this way for very long.

Sylvia asked if he wanted her to leave the ship and come home. He said, "Wait a while and call me tomorrow morning, and depending on how Tony is, then we could decide what to do." Sylvia agreed.

The next morning, she promptly called his brother. She was willing to leave at a moment's notice. When his brother answered the phone, Sylvia asked how he was doing. He told her, "Tony seemed to be holding his own, but we're not sure. Things could change any time, and Tony was very ill."

Needless to say, Sylvia was extremely worried, but she tried not to show it on the cruise, and made the best of it. The following morning, Sylvia called again and asked the same question. This time, she was informed that they thought Tony seemed to be stable. His brother thought he would be all right until she got home, but would call if there were a change for the worse.

Sylvia completed her cruise and was very glad to be going home. As soon as she landed at the airport, she quickly hailed a taxi, picked up her car, and went to the hospital. When she got there, Tony's oldest brother and wife were there with his younger brother. Tony's oldest brother invited her to stay at their house rather than go to a motel. That is exactly what Sylvia did, because the hospital would no longer let her stay at their lodge. They never expected this to be such a long process. Sylvia declined at first. She hardly knew them and didn't want to impose.

Soon after Sylvia arrived, Tony's family left. She was surprised to see that Tony was in another room, one that was semi-private. She looked for his doctor, and once he was found, she asked to be brought up to date on the happenings while she was away. The doctor explained how Tony had been through some very critical moments. They had found cirrhosis of the liver and, perhaps, cancer of the pancreas when they operated. They weren't sure of the cancer. There definitely was something wrong with the organ, but they didn't have time to investigate further.

Sylvia couldn't understand how Tony got cirrhosis of the liver. He didn't drink. After all, before his quintuple bypass, when they gave him the CAT scan, there was no sign of cirrhosis. All they found were stones in his bladder and an enlarged prostate. Then she remembered what the doctor at the Boston hospital told her about their blood-screening perfection—the implication being that Tony must have been given bad blood previously. She then knew why they shipped him back to the VA Hospital. They obviously didn't want to be entangled in a lawsuit, and decided to send him back to where the problem probably originated.

The next day, when Sylvia went to visit Tony, he was no longer in the semi-private room. He had been moved to a ward. Tony was being fed via an intravenous drip and was given no whole food. At one point, the intravenous needle had come out of its position and Tony wasn't taking in any nourishment. Sylvia called a nurse and asked if she would re-insert the needle. Sylvia was told that the nurse could not do this, that a technician was the only one who could do this procedure.

Sylvia then told her to get the technician. What was so hard about figuring that out? With this, Sylvia was told that the technicians had gone for the weekend. This meant that Tony had no nourishment all weekend long.

She would go out and get him some soup, so that he could have something, but Tony was getting weaker and weaker. To top it all, Sylvia found out there was a patient in the ward who had pneumonia. A day or two later, another pneumonia patient arrived. Tony, being so run down after his operation, soon contacted the pneumonia.

Sylvia was furious and accused the doctors and nurses of neglect. They suggested putting Tony in a nursing home for twenty-four-hour care, but Tony did not want to go. Sylvia raged that no nursing home was equipped to deal with Tony's multiple problems; the hospital was. They were responsible and they were to get him better. But Tony was without the intravenous drip several more times, and he was getting weaker still.

She brought him food to eat from time to time, but the doctors had her stop feeding Tony because he might choke. The doctors and nurses were also giving him more and more morphine. Sylvia called Tony's family together and suggested they talk to the doctors and tell them they wanted Tony to have more nourishment, less morphine, and wanted him removed from the ward. The family agreed.

When they had the meeting with the doctors, they made their demands. Surprisingly, it went fairly well. They finally took Tony out of the ward, put him in a semi-private room, and gradually reduced the morphine.

When Tony was more lucid, it seemed he had harbored some resentment toward Sylvia about her trip. He said that his family stuck together, and since she came back, he hadn't seen much of her. Sylvia was sorely hurt by these remarks, but thought how was he supposed to know she was there when he was knocked out on morphine every day? That day, when Tony's younger brother, George, got to hospital, Sylvia begged George to please, tell Tony that she had been there every day since she came home. George looked at Tony and told him, in no uncertain terms, she had been there every day for hours on end.

As Tony got more nourishment, his body functioned more normally. He asked Sylvia to get the nurse because he needed a bedpan. At first, Sylvia put on the call light for a nurse, but no one came. Finally, she went out on the floor, saw a nurse, and asked if she would get a bedpan for Tony. The nurse said he would have to wait because she was busy. Sylvia stood there watching—all the nurse was doing was standing over a tray of supplies, doing nothing.

Sylvia repeated three times that a bedpan was needed. Still, the nurse wouldn't move. Sylvia got so upset that she went back in the room and told Tony to do whatever he had to do, and she would make the nurse clean it up. After Tony was through, Sylvia called the nurse and ordered her to clean him and the whole bed.

The doctors and nurses only did what his family and Sylvia wanted for three or four days, then went right back to their old routine of utter neglect. At one point, Tony looked at Sylvia in anguish and said, "I am going to die." Sylvia said, "Yes, but just think, you will be with God in heaven for all eternity. You will shed your old, decayed body and have a new one. You will be a new creation, and when God decides to take me home, we will be together for eternity." The anguish in his face disappeared, and a beautiful, peaceful calm came over him.

The following day, when Sylvia entered the hospital, Tony was no longer in the semi-private room, but in a private room. Sylvia thought it was a good sign of something. Little did she know.

As if things weren't bad enough, yet another complication arose. Sylvia had been, at the time, renting a beautiful home in Groton for the last two and a half years. On March 15, she received a call from her landlord, telling her the house was to be sold, and he wanted her out by the end of the month. With everything else going on, that was impossible. She explained the situation with Tony and he relented a bit, asking how much time she needed. She told him until May 1, and he agreed.

She immediately contacted a few brokers, and after looking at five houses, settled on one in Westford. It was a split-level house, about thirty years old, which sat in the middle of a nursery growing trees and shrubs. It was smaller than the house in Groton, but it could hold all of her furniture, so she rented it. The more she thought about it, the more she liked the idea of living in such a nice, private place within a nursery.

Chapter 25

It was now approximately May 1, 2000. Tony had been in the hospital for nearly two full months. Sylvia again complained to the doctor about making sure Tony received proper nourishment. The doctor seemed a bit frustrated. She said that every time she tried to talk to the family, they told her to talk to Sylvia. She couldn't understand that the bond Sylvia and Tony had was a bond that had lasted fifty-five years so far. But the family knew, and they gave Sylvia all the authority they felt she should have. Sylvia was very surprised at what was happening; she never expected the complete relinquishing of authority to her.

Very often, Sylvia would ask Tony where he wanted her to sleep at night. She would leave the hospital about 10:00 PM. She was afraid to go home because it was an hour's ride. She would opt to stay at a motel, or stay at his brother and sister-in-law's house. When she asked Tony what he wanted her to do, he would always tell her to go to his brother's house. They welcomed her with open arms.

One time when they were giving Tony less morphine, Tony had a nightmare. He was yelling and waving his arms all over the place. Sylvia tried waking him and holding him to calm him down. When he woke up and saw Sylvia and realized he had had a nightmare, he told Sylvia he dreamt he was falling. She assured him everything was all right, but at this point, she felt maybe a little sedative would help quiet him down. She told the doctor that she thought that he needed a little sedative. That's all they needed to hear; they quickly put him on morphine again.

That evening, while he was sleeping, Sylvia was standing by his bed. Cold air was being vented into the room right over his bed. This vent had nothing to do with the air conditioning system that could be monitored and controlled. Sylvia called the nurse and showed her that cold air was being piped in, and asked if it could be shut off. The nurse said she didn't know where it was coming from, and there was no one around who could do anything about it. The next day, Sylvia again demanded that he be fed intravenously. They gave him nourishment and looked at Sylvia very grudgingly.

After that evening of cold air being blown over Tony, needless to say, he was in worse condition the next morning. She had tried to put more blankets on him the previous evening to keep him warm. That morning, when Sylvia arrived, Tony looked at Sylvia and told her they had put him through hell. They worked on him all morning, sticking tubes down his throat. When the doctor came in, right away, she called Sylvia out into the corridor. She told Sylvia that Tony had a bowel movement that morning, and that it was full of blood, so, with Tony's permission, they explored inside to find the cause. Sylvia asked Tony, if indeed, he did give them permission to explore. He said he did not. At this point, he was so fragile, and had lost so much weight, an examination like that did a great deal of harm.

On March 1, when Tony first went into the hospital, he weighed 108 pounds; way down from his normal 180 pounds. He was now at about seventy-five pounds. He was convinced they were doing him no good. In the middle of the night, he tried to get out of bed. In his mind, he wanted to get out of the hospital, just like he escaped the tuberculosis hospital years before. Needless to say, he was far too weak. The nurses found him on the floor and put him back in bed.

Tony's sister-in-law asked him if he gave permission to the doctors to stick tubes down his throat, and he definitely said no. To make matters worse, two days later, on the weekend, another group of doctors did the same thing. Sylvia complained to the first doctor and told her that they went inside him again over the weekend. The first doctor knew nothing of the second round of internal examinations. She asked the doctor who was in charge on the weekend to investigate. At Sylvia's demand, she admitted that it was true.

When Sylvia went back into Tony's room, she was obviously very upset. Tony looked at Sylvia and said they were experimenting on him. This time, he said it in an accepting way, as if to say that he was dying anyway, so they now wanted to use him for experimentation.

That evening, when Sylvia entered the hospital, Tony was again heavily sedated by the morphine, and his face looked very peaceful and calm. Every day when Sylvia would visit him, she had a habit of testing his senses. She would put her hand in his and ask if he knew she was there. Most times, he could feel her hand and would clasp his hand to hers. This time, he was lying on his side and his hand was in a half-open position. Sylvia put her hand to his, but there was no response. Sylvia stood watching him, lying there so peacefully and breathing. His breaths were very calm and regular. After quite some time, at 7:10 PM, Sylvia could see no point in staying. He didn't even know she was there. She went home, and at about 8:40 PM, she received the unwanted call from the doctor. Tony had expired at 8:30 PM.

Sylvia's heart was broken, but in a way she was relieved. He had suffered so much for so long. Now he was at peace with the Lord. Sylvia called the brothers and informed them of his death, and gave them the time of death. They asked if she was there when he died. She told them that he was unresponsive and seemed to be resting very comfortably, and she had not stayed. Later, the hospital called Sylvia again and asked if she would allow an autopsy. Sylvia insisted they were to leave the body alone.

Sylvia remembered that Tony always said he wanted to have a veteran's burial in a veterans' cemetery. Sylvia called the office of the burial grounds at Fort Devens, and asked if there was room at the cemetery for a veteran. They replied that no more plots were available, but did have space if she wanted to have the body cremated.

The family met with Sylvia, expressing that they would like her input in making arrangements. She told them of his desire to be buried as a veteran, and about her call to Devens. The family, being staunch Catholics, did not like the idea of a cremation, even though the Catholic Church allows them now.

His sister Gingy offered to have him buried in a plot she purchased for her husband. There would be room there for Tony as well. They chose the same funeral home all of the family had used in the past.

Sylvia had purchased some new clothing earlier, hoping that these would be the clothes he would wear when he got well and came home. She had no idea they would be his burial clothes. She had purchased a shirt, underwear, and socks. The brother provided the suit, tie, and shoes from Tony's wardrobe at home.

Tony's sister-in-law asked Sylvia if she thought the casket should be closed because he had lost so much weight. Sylvia told her there was no need to have a closed casket. He had a very peaceful look on his face when she last saw him.

The following day, the family asked Sylvia to go to the funeral home with them to make all the arrangements. From here on, the family made it plain that if the directors of the funeral home had any questions, they were to speak with Sylvia directly. Sylvia wrote the announcement that was to be given to the newspapers:

May 16, 2000, Age 70. A World War II disabled veteran. A volunteer for over a decade for Sylvia's Haven (a transitional shelter for homeless women and their children) at Devens, MA.

Anthony would take the women and children to hospitals and clinics, when needed. Provided transportation for shopping, job interviews, and made frequent trips to Boston Food Bank for the Haven. Was responsible for packing 85 percent of 32 truckloads of furnishings and clothing and transporting them to the Haven without cost. Over 300 women and children will miss this kind-hearted servant of the Lord.

The undertaker was given the write-up for the newspapers and asked who wrote it. Sylvia admitted to the task.

The family and Sylvia went to pick out the casket and flowers. The visiting hours were on Friday from 2:00 to 4:00 and 7:00 to 9:00 PM. Sylvia was given the first seat next to the casket, as though she was his wife. The family showed every respect for her. It was as if Tony instructed them to do so.

One of the people who took his death the hardest was Peter's daughter. (Peter is Sylvia's Haven's treasurer.) Her mother told Sylvia she had cried for two weeks.

Tony's sister Marie came in with her husband and daughter. This was the first time in forty-seven years that Sylvia and Marie laid eyes on one another. Marie approached Sylvia and cried. She stayed with her most of the evening. What a shame that it took his death to bring these two women together. Marie was truly sorry for separating herself from Sylvia and Tony, and her tears showed it. Now

Tony was dead and she couldn't apologize to him. This, Sylvia thought, was truly why she cried so much.

Sylvia met the nieces and nephews. Six of whom she had never met before, and the other three she had only known as children from three to five years of age. Now they were in their upper forties and fifties.

The following morning, the day of the burial, Sylvia and the family were picked up by the funeral limousine and taken to say goodbye for the last time with family and friends. Marie arrived, and again tears flowed down her face. Before they closed the casket, she went over and kissed Tony on the forehead. When they left the funeral home, Sylvia was the first to be seated behind the hearse. When they arrived at the church, they asked for pallbearers. Two of his brothers, three of his nephews, and Sylvia's oldest son volunteered to escort the body down the aisle.

Sylvia gave the eulogy. She told everyone about Tony, the man she knew and his family didn't. She spoke of the work he did over the past thirteen years, the way he taught himself to play the piano, and the caring person he was to homeless women he had never met before but served willingly, without thought of reward. He just simply gave from his heart. Later, one of his brothers told her he didn't even know his own brother.

After the church service, Sylvia was again given the place of honor in the first limousine. After the burial, Tony's sister-in-law invited everyone to come to her house for fellowship and food. Tony's sister Marie didn't go to the house or even the burial, because her husband got separated from the funeral party and didn't know his way to the cemetery. Discouraged and upset, he just returned home. Marie was very upset over this incident and called Tony's sister-in-law, apologizing and crying. This only compounded Marie's sorrow.

After things had settled down a bit, Sylvia asked Tony's brother, "May I go through Tony's wallet to get pictures of my family." She knew what he had in his wallet (or so she thought). Its contents would mean nothing to his family. Tony's brother quickly obliged. When Sylvia looked through his wallet, she found much more than she expected. He had her children's pictures; that she expected. He also had the very seductive picture of Sylvia taken when she was twenty-one. It had now been in his wallet for fifty years.

There was another item that was a total surprise to Sylvia. It was a typewritten letter, carefully folded so that the print was on the inside. It was folded down to a piece of about one and a half inches by two inches. It was her letter breaking it off with Tony in favor of Rick. When Sylvia read the letter, she thought maybe he had saved the letter until the day he died as a reminder of why she left him for Rick.

Tony's brother asked her if she would like some of the greeting cards she had given him over the years. He said he threw out a big pile of them, but gave her the remaining few. She began to compile a scrapbook with those cards and others she had saved over the years.

As time went on, Tony's sister-in-law showed Sylvia their family album. Sylvia asked if she might borrow some of the pictures to duplicate for her album. She was very obliging, and soon, Sylvia was well on her way to having an album solely of Tony, Sylvia, and his family. During this time, Sylvia would be invited to different community and family affairs on the weekend. It grew to the point that Sylvia stayed over at their house every weekend.

One evening, Sylvia experienced what she described as an appearance by Tony. She documented the following in her diary:

"September 17, 2000 – I woke up about 1:30 AM, fell back to sleep at approximately 3:30 AM. I dreamed Tony and I were in a car and I was driving. Location – the North End of Boston, right outside of the Callahan Tunnel. We were heading toward the entrance of the tunnel. As I was driving, Tony was kissing me. I was driving very slowly. The kisses were the most tender, loving kisses I had ever had. He was holding my face and kissed me about 5 times.

"As I was entering the tunnel, I was trying to be very careful of our safety. There were two bikes lying down on the pavement on the side of the entrance to the tunnel. I missed them and turned the vehicle around so as to position myself to an opening past the bikes. All the while Tony was kissing me. When I was about fifteen feet from the entrance to the tunnel, I woke up. The fear of hitting the bikes jarred my sleep and I sat up in bed. Immediately after I sat up, I heard Tony's voice in an audible, gentle, low sweet tender voice just above a whisper, saying, 'See.'

"At first, I thought it was a word of a sentence, which had been broken and 'See' might have been 'Sea.' But quickly I realized the 'SEE' had a great many meanings. One possible meaning might be: 'See, even though you moved when I was in the hospital and I never saw your new home, here I am able to find you and still be with you.' The second possible meaning could be: 'See how much I love you.' And the third: 'See? Look at me, I have a whole new body that will never deteriorate.' It could have been all of the above.

"He looked as he did when he was 35. This experience is the most precious experience I have ever had in my life."

Three months later, Sylvia had another such experience. She recorded it as follows:

¬"December 15, 2000 – I went on a junket with Tony's younger brother George last evening. The bus returned at 1:OO AM. Rather than go home so late, Tony's sister-in-law suggested I sleep at her apartment on the second floor of Tony's house. It was a three-story building occupied solely by his family.

"I woke up about 4:00 AM and fell asleep again at approximately 5:30 AM. I dreamed I was in a large home similar to an expensive executive home, which had two stories. It apparently was Tony's home but I felt it was his new home in heaven. It seemed as though there were at least six members of the family present. We all seemed very happy. There was Tony's brother Sam, who is deceased, his sister Marie, still with us and in the background, I sensed his brother and sister-in-law. There was music playing and I called to Tony, 'Tony, come on down. I want to dance with you.' Tony appeared at the top of the stairway on the second floor and came down and danced with me.

"Tony was not an exceptionally good dancer but I would call him an amateur who did a sort of generic dance most men do in ballrooms. In the flesh, Tony would have appeared awkward, conscious of his inability to dance like a professional. But in the spirit, there was no sense of awkwardness, merely an all-encompassing love, holding me and slowly moving his feet to the beat of the music. Love seemed to pour out of him from every pore, with a deep spiritual love. I felt so completely protected in his arms. When the dance ended so did the dream."

One year after Tony's death, in May of 2001, his brother and sister-in-law were discussing the fact that an anniversary Mass should be said for Tony. Sylvia agreed. Mel and Sylvia went to the church to make the arrangements, and Sylvia paid for the Mass. Mel then proceeded to notify the family. Some of the members of the family could not attend because they had to work. One of them was Tony's nephew, Mark. He was the first grandchild born to the family.

Tony and Mark were very close. Although Mark couldn't attend, he made sure his wife Cheryl did. After the service was over, Cheryl approached Marie and Sylvia and apologized for Mark's absence. One evening, Mark called Sylvia and spoke with her for quite some time. He told her that he had possession of his mother's family photograph album and was glancing through it after his uncle died. He saw a picture of a young girl riding a bike, with the caption "Sylvia" at the bottom. He told her there was also a photo of his uncle Anthony, as he called him, obviously taken on the same day on the same bike. He said the picture of Sylvia was always there, but they never knew who she was or why the photo was there.

He began talking about "Uncle Anthony" and explained how he was his favorite uncle. As he began talking about how he admired him so, his voice began to choke up. Sylvia could sense the tears in his eyes. She asked if she might borrow the pictures. He told her he would not only send those two pictures, but would include others he thought she might like.

When Sylvia received the pictures, she quickly had them copied, and called to thank him. He invited her to his home for a cookout. They had a wonderful time talking about "Uncle Anthony."

Sylvia now visits with the family each weekend and has become an integral part of the family.

An entire era had come to an end. There is no doubt this patient, kind, giving man was the major love of her life.

But, before his passing, other things were afoot.

A composite of the two "bike" pictures.

Chapter 26

On the day of completion of Devens' phase one, there was a grand opening, complete with ceremony. The day before, the police contacted Sylvia and told her they found a girl walking in the rain on the highway, with a tiny baby and asked if she would take her in. Sylvia was pleased to be able to help. She was her first client at Devens.

During the open house, the press was very favorable with its coverage, and they took pictures of the event, including pictures of the first resident and her baby. It wasn't long before all fourteen townhouses were filled with clients and their children, except for one that Sylvia took for an office.

The clients could not believe they had a whole house to themselves. Some never lived in such a home before. The twenty-plus acres of property made for a beautiful setting. The families had their own private community, and the children had ample room to play.

Sylvia's daughter Lynda became her first executive assistant. She was so excited to be made a part of the ministry that she, on top of her office duties, took it upon herself to set up the first three houses with furniture and everything else that the clients might need. To keep expenses as low as possible for Sylvia's Haven, Lynda was given a townhouse, as were all future employees. In so doing, wages could be kept low for the organization, and there would be people on site 24/7.

The length of stay for each client was set at two years. During this time, the client would be assisted and directed to a place of education. If it was felt the client needed counseling, she was referred to the Lipton Center, a large and diverse organization providing substance-abuse programs, support groups, sexual-assault programs, mental healthcare and counseling on an outpatient basis. At one point, a counselor actually set up an office at Devens and would spend one day a week to help clients of Sylvia's Haven. When it came time for them to find a job, there was assistance there as well. Finally, they were assisted in finding permanent housing. Unfortunately, they were made so comfortable that, at times, they didn't want to leave The Haven, and Sylvia had to resort to the court system to force them out for dragging their heels.

Clients were never sent out on the streets with nothing to their names. They already had a Section 8 housing certificate, and Sylvia always made certain they had an established permanent place to go. They were also allowed to take with them all of the possessions accumulated: furniture, clothing, dishes, cookware, everything. When they set up their permanent home, they wanted for nothing.

Two years into the project, Lynda got engaged, and wanting to get on with her life, left The Haven. Sylvia always wanted to hire from within, and thought that one of her charges, Grace, would be a good choice. She was separated from her husband and had three children, and Sylvia noticed she was very intelligent. Occasionally, Grace's husband, Ralph, would visit the children and, eventually, Grace and he reconciled. When she told Sylvia of a probable reconciliation, she asked Sylvia if Ralph could apply for the full-time maintenance job that was now available. Sylvia interviewed him and thought it would be a good arrangement, Grace in the office and Ralph as the maintenance supervisor.

It was about this time that Sylvia managed to complete phase two of her remodeling plan. Mass Development would give her a listing of improvements to be made to each townhouse before they would issue an occupancy permit. One of the last steps in the renovation process was to install and test a sprinkler system. Once tested and passed, the permit would be issued, and Sylvia had complete freedom to use the facility as she wished.

As the organization grew (phase two brought twelve more townhouses online), Sylvia had to take one of the new units as additional office space. She moved her office to the new unit, and she made her old office available for Grace, complete with a reception area and computer room.

Although planned for phase five, it was necessary to spend more than $20,000.00 on repairs for the chapel, as related earlier, not only for building maintenance but for the cost of utilities to keep the building warm enough so that pipes didn't burst. Further repairs were put on hold.

Now, about two years later, phase three was completed. Sylvia waited for the fire chief to come, inspect the property, and give her that all-important certificate of occupancy. When she got it, the sixteen additional units brought the total to forty units available for occupancy.

Grace and Ralph had worked out well for more than four years. They had saved every penny they could, and finally decided to buy a home of their own. Ralph returned to his previous profession as an EMT. His brother, who had been assisting Ralph, was made supervisor.

At the same time, Teddie and Cathy needed a new apartment. Their old one was in a home that had recently been sold, and the new owners were taking the rents up to prevailing market rates. That meant the $600.00 they were paying would be increased to an unreachable $1,200.00. Sylvia decided that she would hire Cathy (she had office experience and worked as a secretary in Morocco) and gave them one of the townhouses to live in, just as every other employee. All things considered, it was a financial match. Teddie got a local job, Cathy worked in the office, at a lesser rate of pay, but with many other perks, it all worked out well.

After phase three was completed, Sylvia began the task of bringing the last ten buildings up to code. When they were 80 percent done, she was informed that the Agency wanted to move her to a different location. With that prospect, in the future, she was told to halt all construction.

Unfortunately, the move was not to be, and a lawsuit was brought about, which is a matter of record at the Federal Court, located in Boston.

The lawsuit lasted nearly four years. All this time, however, Sylvia never stopped operating her ministry. By 2006, she had sheltered 993 women and children.

As mentioned before, the fifty houses she chose were townhouses. Each family lived in one whole townhouse. Sylvia's Haven would fill the homes with everything they needed: furniture, appliances, dishes, pots, pans, linens and all. When the women got on their feet and were able to leave, they were given all of the furnishings. By the time they left, they had a fully furnished home and a job, and were on their way to a fresh start.

The pending lawsuit hurt the donations to the Haven greatly, because of a bogus smear campaign led by her landlord to justify her eviction. Sylvia had to start borrowing on her five credit cards to pay expenses and payroll. That jeopardized her credit. Paying rent for the houses she used for her personal residences over the years had also depleted all of her resources. Over a period of eight years, she had paid out more than $200,000 in rent. The Haven, by agreement of her board, gave her this housing allowance, but with donations coming in at various rates, for the most part, they were inadequate to reimburse her.

She decided, she had to prepare the section of the chapel designated in the proposal as her residence. She had to move out of her latest rented house soon or face eviction.

The first thing she had to do was deal with the massive boiler. She decided to replace it with three smaller units so the space could be zoned. In the summer of 2004, a plumber was hired to install the one unit that would heat her future space. Sylvia outlined what he was to do. When the plumber went to get the building permit, he must have been told to alter her plans. She wanted two sets of baseboards on each side of her unit, instead he put one row of baseboards on one side and ran the other across about one third of the way across the chapel. Thereby heating some of the chapel, and leaving Sylvia with only half of what she needed for heating. Obviously, before they would allow him the permit this is the arrangement made by her landlord. Sylvia paid $12,000.00 for the job and could have sued both the plumber and her landlord, but there was already a law suit pending with her landlord. Sylvia wanted no further problems with them, and halted the rest of the construction at the chapel.

She devised an alternative by using two side-by-side townhouses. One would have been too small for her furniture. She had her new maintenance supervisor, Jim, make passageways from one unit to the other on the first and second floors. In one case, an entire wall had to be taken out to create a room large enough to fit her bedroom set. Jim was hired part time initially, but worked out so well, Sylvia made him full time and let go another part-timer. Somehow, the work was completed, and she finally moved in so she could live rent-free.

As for the Devens property, it was always well maintained by Jim. The lawns were properly mowed, snow was plowed as soon as it fell, and rubbish was being handled by Waste Management at a cost of over $800.00 per month. Jim approached Sylvia and said she could save money by having Jim pick up the trash that was kept out of sight, twice a week. It could be brought to the dump in Harvard, since she was officially occupying property in the town of Harvard, the cost $200.00, for using the dumping facility per year. Compared to a cost of over $9,000.00 annually for Waste Management, Sylvia was very grateful to Jim for saving her this kind of money, and he did a wonderful job. She was even approached by an officer of the State Police, who complimented her that there had never been a problem with her operation, clients, or property.

During this period of time, one evening Sylvia was going out for a few hours. Although it wasn't late, it was already dark. For some unknown reason her right knee seemed to have locked, Sylvia couldn't move. She didn't know what to do. There she was in the middle of a nursery and seemingly no one around.

Suddenly, she heard the howling of wolves. It seemed as though they knew there was an injured person there. Luckily her van was no more than two feet away. Sylvia was so frightened, even with the excruciating pain managed to get in the van. There were caretakers on the property that lived a few hundred feet away. She thought to herself, "I'll try to see if anyone is home."

As she approached their driveway, she noticed their truck leaving the house. She parked her van across their driveway blocking their way, to get attention. One of the men got out of the truck and asked Sylvia if anything was wrong. She told them she couldn't move. They called the ambulance and it brought her to the local hospital.

She was there three days and they could not determine what went wrong. On the third day, they tried to have her walk. She was able to walk only about 10 feet and they returned her to bed. They decided to send her to a rehabilitation facility close to where she lived.

Slowly they had her walking longer distances. Then they had her try to climb stairs, because in order for her to be sent home she would have to climb about 10 steps. It took about a week, and then they discharged her. Jim came to see Sylvia every day and on the day she was to go home he picked her up. For about two weeks, Jim drove her everywhere she needed to go. They joked, it was like "Driving Miss Daisy." Again, God came through and provided Jim for help.

Chapter 27

❧

Phyllis's Story – To the Devens Project

On February 1990, while in the care of Life for the Little Ones, Phyllis gave birth to a beautiful baby girl she named Renee'.

Phyllis was born in Nigeria, the daughter of a wealthy family. There seems to be a large number of similar families who follow the same scenario with their children. When a woman was pregnant and about to give birth, they would go to England to deliver, therefore becoming an English citizen. Eventually it was common to return to the U.K. to live. But after the birth, the mother and child would return to Nigeria. When it was time for the child to go to school, an exclusive private school was chosen that catered to the rich. When they completed their schooling in Nigeria, the parents would send them to the U.S. to attend Mount Ida College in Newton, Massachusetts. At least two families, from different towns in Nigeria, followed this path.

Founded in 1899, Mount Ida was a private women's high school; by 1967, they offered their first associate degree program. In the 1980s it became co-ed and had a junior and senior college division.

Phyllis was there as part of her education, and began dating a young countryman of the same ilk. While both were from Nigeria, they had grown up in different towns and had met only after arriving at Mount Ida. As with all of Sylvia's clients, Phyllis became pregnant. In her case, however, she twice tried aborting the baby. After the second attempt failed, she felt that God was protecting the child. She sought out and found Life for the Little Ones and carried the baby to full term. On February 20, 1990, little Renee' was born.

The father at first, vowed he would stay with Phyllis, and even baby-sat while she looked for employment. But the relationship would never get any stronger, and finally ended.

Early on in the month of May 1990, Phyllis asked Sylvia if her mother could visit and stay for a while. When she said her mother would be willing to sleep on a mattress on the floor, Sylvia thought it would not be that much of an imposition,

128

and agreed to the visit. At the time, Sylvia was housing her clients in a single-family house. They shared all of the other rooms, but had private bedrooms.

As it turned out, Phyllis's mother arrived toward the end of May, just as Sylvia was about to enter the hospital for her cancer surgery. She visited Sylvia two or three times during her stay, but her efforts at the house really shined through. Without being asked, she took over the role of resident manager after Kristine left, cooking for the women and cleaning the common areas. Everyone loved her. She stayed at the house right up until September.

Then the weather, getting ever colder, got to be too much for her, and she felt it was time to return home. Phyllis had enrolled herself in a cosmetic school, so her mother suggested she take baby Renee' back to Nigeria so Phyllis could get on with her life. Of course, Phyllis could see the baby any time she wished. Plane fare would be provided. Phyllis agreed. She found out later that her mother and father called in designers to their estate to make a nursery for the new arrival.

But while her mother was still in the States, she tried to get in touch with Renee's grandparents. Through some inquiries, she learned that her sister lived in the same Nigerian town as the father's parents. Armed with this information, the father's mother was contacted. She not only rebuffed the contact, but claimed Phyllis had ruined her son's life. No marriage was to take place.

As Renee' grew, she followed the same educational path as Phyllis, going to the same private school. She was an extremely bright, intelligent, and beautiful young girl, and at the age of thirteen won a teen beauty contest. Her grandmother sent photographs to Sylvia of the reigning queen. As to how bright Renee truly was, she skipped grades three times, and by the age of sixteen, was ready to enter college.

Her father had obviously been tracking the progress of his daughter. He very much wanted to be a part of her life, as he always had, and bring her to the U.S. Phyllis and Renee' were living in the U.K. at the time. Knowing that a life in the States would be better for her, she agreed to let Renee's father take her there, the land of her birth.

It had now been sixteen years since Sylvia had seen the baby that now was a beautiful young woman. Renee' and her grandmother were coming in from Nigeria. When they arrived, the grandmother phoned Sylvia. The father greeted them at the airport. Sylvia was very excited to see them once again and took them to a very nice restaurant for lunch. They all had a warm and loving reunion. The father was living with a woman who had a son about seventeen years of age. Sylvia was afraid this could spell trouble. He had paid for the airfare from Nigeria, and later enrolled Renee' in a local community college.

Sylvia had one very enjoyable trip with Renee' to Newport, Rhode Island, touring the area and the mansions there: The Marble House, a summer home for the Vanderbilts; Kingscote, built also as a summer home by a Southern plantation owner in a gothic style; The Elms, commissioned by a rather obscure coal magnate from Pennsylvania; Rosecliff, built by a naval historian and diplomat, later bought and expanded by a Nevada silver heiress; and of course, the greatest of the summer cottages (read incredibly large and opulent) called The Breakers.

The father, from then on took complete control of rearing his daughter. The woman he was living with took her son and left. She felt she couldn't compete with his daughter

It is somewhat ironic that the current office of Sylvia's Haven is located in Revere, Massachusetts. It is in a twelve-story building, right on Revere Beach Boulevard, no more than 100 yards from the ocean. There is nothing in between but a two-lane road, a sidewalk, and an expansive beach. The building is named The Breakers.

Renee' entered college and completed her associates degree. At that point, Renee's mother and grandmother came to the United States to be with her for her granduation. Her father let them stay at his house for the festivities. Renee's mother had married many years ago and had a daughter about 12 years of age and a son about 10 years of age. They came to see their sister, also.

After they arrived, they contacted Sylvia and invited her to come for the celebration, Sylvia gladly went. She took them to Rockport, to spend the afternoon. Everyone enjoyed themselves. Sylvia asked Renee' what were her plans for the future, she replied she would go back to school for her MBA. Sylvia was very pleased. About two years later, Renee's grandmother spoke to Sylvia and told her Renee' had changed her mind and was going to college to become a lawyer. Renee' is now twenty-one years of age.

Chapter 28

For nearly four years, the lawsuit was pending. In 2005, the lead attorney of Sylvia's battery of attorneys had an aid whose job included daily trips to the statehouse, to monitor what was going on legislatively. The aid was very friendly with one particular state representative by the name of Paul Loscocco. Mr. Loscocco was also an attorney; an extremely intelligent man who graduated magna cum laude. The aid told Rep. Loscocco about Sylvia's case, and asked the representative would he be willing to read the file. Rep. Loscocco agreed. The aid, gave him a copy of the case material, and asked him to render any assistance he could.

Sylvia's lawyer then informed Sylvia that Rep. Loscocco, after reading the case, agreed to help. Sylvia was surprised because he wasn't even in her district. The first thing he did was go to Devens to try to convince the TRA to drop the suit. They completely ignored him.

In 2006, when the state's budget was being put together, Paul started an awesome campaign. He contacted all of the top men in the governor's office, bringing them up to speed on what was going on. He also contacted the chair people of each of the legislative committees, doing the same. Paul then inserted a line item in the State's budget for a grant to Sylvia's Haven, which passed both houses.

Sometime later, a proposal to settle the case out of court was put on the table. It turned out that Paul Loscocco had been successful in his campaign.

Financially, she had no choice. Because of the lack of funds, she had drawn no salary for more than ten weeks. Living off of her social security payment, she even had to round up every bit of change she could find to pay her help. Somehow she managed to pay her staff, but had little else. The settlement was not nearly what it should have been. But rather than prolong the agony any longer, Sylvia accepted. An agreement was signed on August 11, 2006. It stipulated that she had to be out within thirty days.

Knowing she had practically no time, Sylvia began looking for a new home for herself, for the office, and for the girls. The stipulation was that the settlement money would be put in escrow with her lawyers, and not given to her until the organization had physically moved from Devens. Therefore, without the money, Sylvia's hands were tied and she couldn't get anything.

The move out date was September 11, 2006. The agreement was that she would leave the last fifteen families at Devens, and that another shelter, Our Father's House, would take over the care of those families. Upon visiting the Haven, they were overwhelmed and had no conception as to how the Haven could operate. They were used to true shelters with only cots provided for the homeless. Also, the families lived in whole townhouses, completely furnished. The agreement also stipulated that the families would be provided equal or better accommodations. After their two-year stay, the families could take all of the furnishings and clothing from the townhouse to their new homes. But there was always an excess of these donated items. On the move-out date, there were twelve townhouses full of various furnishings. The agreement also stipulated that Sylvia would leave all of the furnishings there, and the fifteen families would keep what was wanted and the TRA would dispose of the rest.

Sylvia took all that she possibly could of her belongings, office materials, and files, and only some of the furnishings that she could use for the new home for the girls. She rented three large storage bins, another added expense that broke her entirely.

She now found herself homeless. For two and a half weeks, she spent three days a week at her sister's home, three days at her sister-in-law's home. On Wednesdays, she took a suite at a hotel at Devens, so that she could work without any interruptions.

While at her sister's home in Revere, Massachusetts, Sylvia looked in the real estate section of the local paper and saw a listing for a condo for rent right next door to her sister's condo building. She called the broker, and within fifteen minutes, she had leased the condo for her home. She then began looking for an adequate office. It had to be quite large to accommodate two offices and a mailroom. So it was back to the newspaper search. She saw a condo that fit the bill, and again called the broker. The one shown was deceiving. Listed as four rooms, in reality it had barely three and a half rooms. Undaunted, Sylvia had the broker contact yet another broker with whom she was working. The second broker knew of another condo in the same building that had four full rooms. She took Sylvia to see it, and it was much more adaptable to what Sylvia needed. The negotiations for this unit took only three days, and it was signed, sealed, and delivered.

Jim was the only employee Sylvia took to Revere from Devens. He now was not only the maintenance supervisor, but through his own suggestion, stated he thought the two of them could also run the office. Now Jim wore two hats among others. Jim didn't know too much about computers, and downloaded all of the directions. He studied and learned quickly, just as he did at Devens.

At Devens when he ran across a situation he knew nothing about, quickly bought a manual that taught him what to do. In the office, he did the same thing.

The condo, in The Breakers, is now being their home office. Sylvia and Jim work side by side every day. It is about one block from where she lived. Jim is now Sylvia's assistant and the Secretary of the Board of Directors.

Now it was time to look for the home for the girls. Prior to moving from Devens, she had looked at properties in the Revere area, and there was only one that she hadn't discounted. She finally felt she had found the home she wanted. It was a thirteen-year-old house with six bedrooms, ideal for the purpose she intended. The former owner had purchased it two years before, but ran into some financial difficulty. After much ado, Sylvia purchased it for the same amount that the previous owner had paid, and papers passed on the evening of December 8, 2006. This property is located about two miles from her home and office, in the Beachmont section of Revere. Things were again falling into place. Sylvia knew, without question, that God had directed everything.

Sylvia was once again starting practically from scratch, because almost everything was left at Devens. With only one couch, a few chairs, a TV and entertainment center, and a microwave stand with no microwave, she had to gather more to complete the home that was to be Sylvia's Haven's new location. She had one new set of dishes, a service for eight, purchased by a donor especially for the Haven. She had about six handmade baby quilts made especially for the Haven. The woman who gave the dishes also purchased new sets of sheets. Soon, Sylvia's bible-study group came to see the house, and each brought linens or money to buy needed items. As soon as the money came in, Sylvia bought whatever it was that the donor designated for the funds. One person bought a new microwave, another, a new iron.

The new house was in excellent condition, but Sylvia could see that in order to accommodate a well-run shelter, some adjustments had to be made. It was a large Cape-style house, built on a steep slope. That made the first floor (up four steps to the front door), and the basement door at the back was actually on ground level.

On an early inspection of the house, she had Jim with her. At this point he had been with her over three years. He opted to move where the job took him, and moved from the Devens area to Revere. Sylvia considers him to be one of the most loyal employees she has ever had. He has done whatever was needed, never refusing a task. Sylvia and Jim literally run the Haven with a few volunteers, part-time employees, and an occasional consultant.

Because the State budget awarded Sylvia's Haven money for needed improvements and office supplies, she looked for things needed to upgrade the office equipment and the house. It seemed the restrictions of the grant did not cover the purchase of new office equipment, only the cost of leasing equipment. Why they would pay up to ten times the cost of purchases in leases remains a mystery, but one deals with what one is presented.

As for the house, Sylvia and Jim needed to inspect it in more detail. While the basement was nearly finished in ceramic tile, she found boxes of tile and hardwood flooring that the previous owner had left. When these boxes were moved to another location, a nice surprise greeted them.

There, in a room that Sylvia thought might make a nice-sized bathroom in the basement, was all the roughed in plumbing required to do exactly that: a flange for a toilet bowl, a drain and supply lines for a sink and tub. She thought a plumber could make short work of the job.

A wooden fence enclosed the front of the property, and it seemed to be in good shape, but on closer inspection, many boards had buckled, presenting possible problems in the future. Sylvia had always looked to the safety of her charges and their children, and had Jim tear out the old fencing. Now there was the problem of how to replace it.

One day, on a ride through Revere, she got a bit lost—no, she found a new way to the client house. Although she had been visiting the area for years, some of the streets remained an enigma to her. She found herself at a "T" intersection, and had to turn left or right. But in front of her was an immaculate white brick home with a short white brick wall in front. A wrought iron railing added about three feet to the wall's height, completing the scene. Passing it off as irrelevant to her current situation, she did still think it was beautiful. She thought she would never be able to afford a wall like that.

But God doesn't think small. When the money became available, she thought of that wall and how it would add to the visual effect of the house. Her insistence on keeping the property neat and tidy during the Devens years, and the positive comments of that officer came to mind now. The nicer her property could be made, the less might be the concerns of the neighbors in the tight New England neighborhood in Revere. She knew that when neighbors found out a shelter had been created there, objections might arise.

In an effort to avoid such objections, even before papers were passed on the property, Sylvia contacted an attorney to get the okay from the City for the new shelter. She got it! She had nearly twenty years of experience with it all, and made a commitment to make the property the best in the neighborhood.

For the second floor to work, Sylvia thought she would have the back wall moved out about twelve feet, and drew up the new configuration herself. She would have to contact the abutters, get their approval, and re-contact the City for its approval. In the meantime, the work on the front of the house, specifically the new wall and railing, could begin.

Contractors were taken to the site and given instructions on how the wall and wrought iron were to be configured. Two were chosen, and work began. Unfortunately, during the construction, a neighbor questioned one of the workers as to what was going on. The worker inappropriately gave out the information that it was to be a home for homeless women and children. That was it. The bomb had dropped. Soon the whole neighborhood learned what was planned, and became alarmed.

At one point during the outside construction, a neighbor approached Jim. Loudly and with much anger, he told Jim that the neighbors were having a meeting, and that they would never move into the new house. Jim knew of the meeting Sylvia and her attorney had set up, and lashed back at the neighbor, saying it was the Haven's meeting.

Feelings were so hard that one neighbor actually twice barged into the house uninvited to see what was going on. The construction workers were surprised to see this interloper glaring at them as they worked. They told Jim of the incursions, and he simply told them to lock the doors so it wouldn't happen again.

Jim didn't know the neighborhood had indeed scheduled its own meeting, and it was to be televised on the local access channel. Of course Sylvia wasn't invited, and found out later that the meeting was rather raucous. They were holding it as a rally to gather opposition to the home, in hopes that public opinion would force Sylvia out.

Less than a week later, Sylvia, her attorney, and Jim attended the planning board meeting. To their surprise, when they walked into the hearing room, there were seventy to eighty people there. The purpose of the meeting was to get the expansion of the second floor approved, but the gathered citizens would soon turn it into a "get Sylvia" party. After the first three speakers had their say, Sylvia's attorney suggested to her that they withdraw the expansion request, thereby removing the purpose of the meeting. It was not anything they had envisioned, and seemed very, very hostile. Nothing could be gained that evening.

The chairman, however, wanted to let more people speak. After all, they had taken the trouble to attend. In any case, the attorney told the board that Sylvia was withdrawing her request.

Rant after rant was voiced. There were even people there from other towns. Sylvia could not believe what was going on. There should have been only abutters there. Speaker after speaker, about ten or so, complained about traffic patterns and the shortage of parking in the area. Had a family moved in, there still might have been the three cars about which she had told the board in her proposal.

Eventually the meeting adjourned. It was all such a waste of time. There would be no vote, as there was nothing to vote on any longer. The neighbors had voiced their opinions, but to no avail. The work at the house continued unabated.

A few weeks later, when the front was done, neighbors started offering compliments on the look of the house. One of the more vocal opponents to the shelter said he thought the expansion was going to go up above the attic and it would have obscured his view of the ocean. Now that the work on the front was done, he thought it added to the neighborhood. Other compliments have been paid, calling the house a work of art and the prettiest house in the area. Other than that, the neighbors have been quiet. Most have become friends, and now give pleasant, quiet greetings when they see Sylvia or Jim. Except for the neighbor next door, who still continuously seems to harass Sylvia, As time goes on, the harassment becomes less and less of a problem.

Chapter 29

Several client stories have been interspersed in this work as examples of how Sylvia's clients came to be, and progressed or failed. Many others have written to her in thanks. Following are just a few of those letters some have written while at the Haven, some after leaving. Of course, names have been changed and some minor editing has been done, but the sentiments are all theirs:

Dear Sylvia Anthony,

I am writing to say thank you for everything that Sylvia's Haven has done for me. The Haven gave me a place to live when I had no place to go.

I came to Sylvia's Haven from my dorm room at Fitchburg State College, and had no place to go eight months pregnant, scared and confused. I couldn't live at school with my son because they didn't have family apartments.

My mother died when I was 19 so I couldn't go live with my parents, because I didn't have any. While at Sylvia's, I have returned back to college at Atlantic Union College. My first semester there I received four A's and an A-. I also got accepted into their nursing program. I will graduate with my associate in nursing (RN), in May of 2006 and my bachelors of a double major of nursing and psychology, in May of 2008.

With the encouragement of Karen, I received a $1,250 scholarship, from the Greater Worcester Community Foundation. This scholarship is renewable for the four years that I will be attending AUC.

I am writing this letter as I am packing to move into my own one-bedroom town house at school. I will miss many of the people that I have become friends with here. I don't know where my son and I would have been if it wasn't for Sylvia's Haven.

Thank you for everything.

Sincerely,
Sandra

To: Everyone it concerns,

I was a client at Sylvia's Haven from April 6th 2003 to May 7th 2004.

I never expected to be treated so well. Everyone went out of their way to treat me and my 2 children Jane and Charles ages 2 and 4. I was given a donated car that helped to give us a way to shop and go to medical appointments.

I am very pleased at how attentive the staff was to our needs and how kind everyone was, all the way until the day I moved.

I'm leaving the Haven to join my husband who serves in the United States Army, after our separation of one year. We've worked on our marriage to make it productive rather than destructive and I truly believe I couldn't have done it without the Haven.

Thank you all, and good luck. You are all loved by my boys and me.

Love, Rose, John and Charles

To whom it may concern:

My name is Ann and I have a 2½-year-old son Gerald.

We became homeless in October 2003. We bounced from a family member's house, to a shelter, to hotels and even more shelters.

When my time was almost up at the last shelter, my advocate at the Boston shelter, found an application for Sylvia's Haven and called on my behalf. Next thing I knew, I had an interview and Mrs. Anthony welcomed my son and me into her shelter with open arms.

I am very thankful for Mrs. Anthony, and I thank God every day for letting us stay here when my son and I were at the end of our ropes.

Yours truly,
Ann and Gerald

Kate's Story

How Did I Get Here? I have been sorting through what is definitely on my mind, fully knowing I never want to go through this again.

As an adult, I worked as an educated, skilled professional for several years and married a man who promised a "normal" marriage. But things got dark and darker until the marriage ended.

In my opinion, the incident that preceded my being here was based upon a work contract violation. The person I was working for was suffering from black-out type rages. He became plainly abusive frequently. Clearly, for a person to have been brought to their knees on these issues alone speaks volumes for their life experience to date.

By the time I came to Sylvia's Haven, I was aghast at the level of violation I had experienced. How wonderful that first night here, I almost sobbed. My assigned housemate gave me a quilt to put over me on her couch in my new room, a second

137

bedroom in the unit where I was sent. I didn't want to shut my eyes it felt so good! Within days, I had a bed, sheets, food, a stove to cook on, and dishes to eat off of: later I was to find clothes.

As a child, my father read stories to me before I went to bed: my favorite was the Red Sea Parting, and I would shiver, and ask my dad: "Will God part the sea if I need it?" Of course, my dad assured me, and I'd hum inside, no words needed!

What is it like now?

Recovery: I've returned to my groups and therapist. My day starts off with Morning Notes, Meditation books, daily calendar things, saying prayers and thinking about the day to come in terms of my behavior matching my values.

Home: I've been moved to a new housemate place, and I'm learning about Sylvia's Haven itself, along with Devens, Ayer and Shirley. The world is expanding and I'm meeting new people. It does not mean that pain is not to follow, my trust issues loom large. Currently, I have resumed working on my artwork. I'm working on projects, Sylvia's library donation painting, Lynda's tri-fold for health fair, and Ayer's First Night Committee, along with substitute teaching have made me enjoy the venture back out.

Living on Devens itself is an unending delight in visual observation, whether it's the geese at Robin Pond, wood duck place on Barnum Road, the hummock on Cold Brook Springs, the perfect pines and birches almost anywhere, and of course, the sandy soil everywhere is just lovely! I've started a painting with some donated paint of a salt marsh on Barnum road, but I could stand almost anywhere, and paint 50 paintings from any point on the circle where I move! Awesome! Truly, the whole town should sigh in awe at this extravagance.

Work: I re-connected with my Boston gallery, Tofias, and they are now carrying the Devens' work too. Christine Dovel, the Director, is such a sympathetic soul to the artist! Sylvia has given me permission to paint in the chapel vestibule (wondrous), and use a room for related work (standard slides, equipment artist's use is really pretty extensive).

In another direction, I was voted by the First Night Committee as Executive Director, and this has re-kindled my marketing skills, my marketing work and I've applied to the Land Bank for a DBA.

What do I hope for?

Being normal, living my life, my value system, and feeling tremendously grateful that for the moment being with people who walk their talk is being in the "Right Place" for now. What a gift, truly! Thank you all who have helped me along the way!

"Kate"

Mary – Written shortly after becoming a client

Before coming to Sylvia's Haven, two months ago I was at what seemed to me rock bottom and I would not see how my life could possibly change for the better. This short piece attests to God's mercies and grace, to the wonderful gift it is to have people like you who choose to help those in need, and Sylvia Anthony's ability to let God lead in her life's work.

I married a man that I had known for several years. Our parents attended the same church and we had been in the same Sabbath school classes. During his work life, he began a relationship with a co-worker. Our lives fell apart and I was left with two wonderful children to raise.

With hardly any support from my husband, our children and I were able to survive with help from my sister and her husband for a while, but the situations we were forced into because of our poverty were horrifying. In 1998, our situation began looking up. It appeared that with a new job, I would be able to cut the cost of childcare, food and other various living expenses. I was also seeing a man who was willing to help with our rent and other needs that arose, which I was unable to cover. I also made the decision that I would keep God's Sabbath and thus not work on Saturday. Also, that I would live my life at a better standard than I ever had before.

Looking back on my life, all of the unbearable hardships have come from making wrong, unsound choices. Choices that were not guided well, but left an unease of conscience. I entered into relationships with men under false assumptions that we loved one another. After vowing to God that I would make changes in my life, I didn't make all of them. I followed what I desired rather than what I knew was right and good.

Then my children were constantly ill. They had the flu and chicken pox back to back. The childcare they attended required that I pay for the month and a half that they were absent. This bill ran over $2,000. That I could not pay as I had been home taking care of my children and thus was unable to work. Throughout this same period of time I had not been feeling well myself. By the time I was able to get back to work I was experiencing fainting episodes, nausea, chest pain, numbness, and tingling in my arms and fingers, abdomen pain and headaches.

I began passing out at work and experienced three episodes where I stopped breathing. My fingers and toes would turn blue and I was sent to emergency rooms unable to speak or move with a pulse that would not register and then would shoot up to 200.

During my last hospital stay, my doctor told me that when I left her office in the ambulance the last time on a stretcher with oxygen and I.V.'s that she believed she would not see me alive again. My relatives came down as soon as my doctor reached them and they began arranging their lives so that they could care for my children. My doctor had advised me to write a living will and this is something I had neglected to do. I did not want to face the severity of my situation.

My sibling told me that when they received the phone call from my doctors and saw me in the hospital they hadn't ever been so scared for my children, herself, and me. My sibling and spouse are all I have for family. I lost my memory, did not know the date, what season we were in or loved ones' names.

A month before ending up at the hospital for the last time, I was lying in my bed wondering what I could read to bring me strength. My bible is what came to mind. It was packed away, but I found it and started poring through its pages. I decided that my life had to metamorphose.

The next day after packing up some groceries I stopped by a store next to the market and saw a wonderful journal with a butterfly on it. It fit right into my thoughts on metamorphosing and I bought it, took it home and started keeping daily notes. I wanted to better maximize my time, eliminate the junk and vain, wasteful persuits and begin doing things right.

After leaving the hospital, my relatives allowed my children and I to stay with them. At the time my doctors wouldn't allow me to work and I didn't know what I would do. I can tell you that I prayed. I began looking for towns with a low per capita income so that I could find low rents and a high per child expense put out for school to ensure a good school system. An opportunity presented itself for my children and I to go live with a friend and I did entertain the thought, however he being male I knew it would eventually lead to difficulties that I could not allow my children to face again.

Then, one morning after a conversation with my relatives, I literally walked into Sylvia's Haven with no idea as to what it was. My prayers were answered. Difficulties still arise. However now I am leaning on God and he promises to grant us strength sufficient to bear all things. This life is better than the life that I attempted to sustain myself.

(Note: Mary now lives in her own home obtained through a USDA Rural Development Grant.)

God has orchestrated, "Life for the Little Ones, Inc." and "Sylvia's Haven, Inc." for over twenty-four years. Sylvia has no reason to doubt that "He will never leave us or forsake us," as promised, and to Him Sylvia gives all the praise and the glory. Sylvia paraphrased from Jabez's Prayer in 1Cronicles 4:10 a personal prayer:

"Oh, that you would bless us indeed and enlarge our territory. That your hand would be with us and that you would keep us from evil. That we may not cause pain, but we may be guided to show love, give hope and security and a future to these women and children, by the Grace of God."

The Father, the Son, and the Holy Spirit still continue to protect and guide Sylvia and Jim. They have had the new home now, over four years. During that time 60 more women and children have been helped. At this writing, the total now helped is 1058 women and children.

Chapter 30

Stephanie's Story – 2007

In April 2007, with the new house's first floor ready for occupancy, Sylvia got a call from Terry, who ran another agency in the area. Terry had a client named Stephanie and her three-year-old baby girl, Tammy. Stephanie was also pregnant, scheduled to deliver on July 4. They were homeless, having been kicked out of her mother's apartment only days before.

The relationship with her mother and sister had been strained for years. About a year before coming to the Haven, her mother told Stephanie she had a week to get out, then changed her mind, saying it was only all of her furniture that was taking up so much room in the apartment. Stephanie called a mover to get the heavy stuff out and into storage. During the few days it was going to take for the movers to arrive, her mother continued to badger her, becoming more and more belligerent and increasingly verbally and psychologically abusive. She told little Tammy that she was eating all of the food Stephanie had brought into the house. That was why Stephanie was leaving. Nothing could have been further from the truth, but what was a three-year-old to believe?

When the movers arrived, the mother told them they were handling stolen goods. Stephanie asked her mother to get her medications and cell phone from her room. She refused and tried to slam the door in her face. Stephanie put her foot in the door, and her mother threw up her hands, screaming that she was being attacked. It was all a show for the movers.

Stephanie decided to call the police, thinking it better to have them arbitrate the hostile situation. In the meantime, her sister had called them. With the police present, her mother and sister brought up all kinds of stories accusingly. They told the cops that she was a thief. It was about an incident when Stephanie was only five. She had nearly walked out of a store with a pack of gum. She was accused of causing her sister to cut her wrists out of frustration, a year or so prior to the move. The police, that time, had come to the apartment at three in the morning to make sure no one else was hurt. They had noticed an awful lot of blood on her sister when she went to the station house.

Tammy was ill that night, and Stephanie needed to clean up a mess she had made. The cleaning supplies were kept in a cabinet in their computer room, then occupied by her sister, but the door was locked. Eventually, Stephanie got a couple of rags and some cleaner and went about her business. Minutes later, her sister went charging into the little girl's room, yelling and screaming about how poorly she was being treated. She said she disowned Stephanie as her sister. Her mother joined in the fray from the next room.

Stephanie eventually got her daughter back to bed, did her homework, and went to bed herself. Her sister must have cut herself sometime during the night, because it wasn't until three in the morning, when the police arrived, that she knew anything about her sister's bloodied wrists.

First thing the next morning, Stephanie was told she and her daughter had three days to leave. Stephanie tried to find a place to stay, but couldn't. Her housing case-worker couldn't help; all the shelters she knew of were full, and the DTA wouldn't take her plight seriously. Her mother changed her mind again and let the two stay on. Stephanie had to apologize (for what, she didn't really know) and do some groveling, but she was grateful to still have a roof over her daughter's head.

That time when the movers finally left, it was very evident that her mother was not going to change her mind again. The police let her stay at the apartment one more night, so she could get the rest of her stuff together. The next night, she and her baby girl slept in her car because every office she had contacted for help was closed. The next day, she was placed in a shelter and had little more than a couple of cots. She desperately hoped she would find better housing soon.

It was then that Sylvia got the call from Terry, and they arranged for an interview with Stephanie. Later that day, when she and her three-year-old daughter arrived, Terry introduced them. Sylvia thought Vera was the cutest little girl, with big blue eyes, and very well behaved. Stephanie filled out an application and was given the Haven's rules. Sylvia reviewed the application and had Stephanie initial each of the rules to make certain they were understood. Stephanie was twenty-six years of age, a disabled veteran who had nerve damage to her arm and hand, and was seven months pregnant with a baby boy. Sylvia thought Stephanie would be a good addition to her home, and decided to take her over to see the new house.

The first thing Stephanie noted was that there were curtains on the windows. She exclaimed, "There are no bars on the windows!" Sylvia asked her why she said that. Stephanie told her that there were bars on the windows of the shelter at which she was staying. The conditions at that other shelter were deplorable, and she wanted to get out. All in all, Stephanie was very impressed with the house, and Sylvia set a move-in date of May 1.

Sylvia had also reached the conclusion that she would have to move into the home. Previously, she had hoped to get a suitable housemother who would be willing to stay at the house full time, including evenings. Evenings are the most important times of all. After a few months of searching, it became apparent that it was not going to be an easy task. Then one night, as she was lying down and thinking about the problem, she felt God telling her something deep in her heart. She should live at the house herself. She had started her shelter with girls in her apartment 24/7, and it seemed as though this was what God wanted now. At least in the evening, she would be there for her girls.

Stephanie and Sylvia moved in on May 1, 2007. Stephanie had a beautiful bedroom, complete with a daybed, youth bed, and a bassinet for the soon to be new arrival.

One day, Sylvia and Stephanie were talking about the pending arrival, and Stephanie was a bit concerned that she had no one to be there for her. Of course, Sylvia told her she would take her to the Beverly Hospital's birthing center when the time came.

At eight o'clock on the morning of July 4, Sylvia heard a knock on her bedroom door. It was Stephanie, and her water had just broken, but she didn't seem to be in any pain. Sylvia started to get dressed, and about fifteen minutes later, she got a call from Jim. He told her Stephanie was on the way to the hospital, but had forgotten a Scooby-Doo tape for Tammy to watch. Jim relayed her request that Sylvia bring it when she came.

Sylvia was shocked. She thought it clear that she would take Stephanie and Tammy to the hospital in her car. Stephanie, not wanting to be too much trouble, drove herself and Tammy in her car.

Sylvia looked unsuccessfully for the requested tape and continued to get ready to go to the hospital. When she arrived around 10 AM, she was told Stephanie was in hard labor and should give birth within the hour. She was asked to wait in the lounge. At 10:27 AM, the seven-pound-eleven-ounce baby boy was born. Sylvia said, "We now have a yankee doodle dandy, born on the fourth of July!" (Referencing the James Cagney classic song in the 1942 film "Yankee Doodle Dandy.) Stephanie named her new baby Anton.

Sylvia has thoroughly enjoyed having a new family in her home. Little Vera loved to play what she called "catch" with Sylvia. When Sylvia would ask for a kiss, Vera would run away from her but to a place she could be caught. Sylvia would pursue her, find her, and kiss her. Vera would giggle the entire time.

When Sylvia gets home in the evening after a day at the office, the first thing she sees is Tammy's little face. She'll stand at the front door and tell her mother that her friend, "the girl" is here. Stephanie told her that she is not a girl, she is "Miss Sylvia." Sylvia told her that being called a girl was fine with her, but she is now Miss Sylvia to Vera.

One day Stephanie invited her best friend to the house for a visit. Her friend also had a daughter not quite two years of age. When Sylvia and Vera started playing "catch", the other little girl, who was more outgoing, hugged Sylvia's thighs and looked up at her, wanting to be part of the game. Sylvia quickly picked her up and kissed her. When Vera saw this she became very jealous. She obviously thought that the new guest was going to steal Sylvia's affection from her.

When Sylvia kissed the little baby, Vera's little face dropped. Sylvia could not help but notice and asked Vera if she wanted to be picked up and kissed. Vera nodded yes. Sylvia quickly picked her up, and Vera threw her arms around Sylvia's shoulders. She began, in a desperate tone, repeating, "I love you, Miss Sylvia, I love you, Miss Sylvia!"

Sylvia kissed her and held her until Vera was assured she was still loved. Sylvia is ever grateful to God for this privilege to serve him through her charges. The joy she has is worth all of the problems that sometime arise.

Sylvia is very pleased with Stephanie. She is already attending college full time, has completed her associate's degree, and is now working on her bachelor's. In fact, she was in school on July 3 and went back, with the baby in tow, on the fifth. Both children are now in day care while Mom is in school.

During this time, Sylvia was invited to speak at her church and tell of her ministry. After she did so, a woman, who had a thirteen-year-old grandson, called to her. Sylvia went over to the lady and was told that her grandson was one of the babies born at the Haven, thirteen years ago. Sylvia is old enough now to enjoy the fruits of her labor.

Now, every Sunday, the teenager will go to Sylvia and kiss her. About a month after the first meeting with the young man, he called to her before the service and said, "I don't remember being born in your shelter. I was too young. But I want to thank you for your hospitality."

If Sylvia had been given a million dollars it would have been nothing compared to what she had experienced. She is constantly reminded of all the reasons the Haven exists.

This young man is now sixteen years of age and plays guitar in the church orchestra. His mother informed her that he is seriously thinking of joining the Air Force as soon as he becomes of age.

Chapter 31

During this time, Jim was now working in the office as Sylvia's assistant and both of them needed someone who was very knowledgeable with computers. Jim had worked at another job with John Griffiths and with Sylvia's permission, asked John if he would be kind enough to help them out.

John graciously obliged. As he was working with them he was gradually familiarizing himself with the history of Sylvia's Haven. At one point, John said to Sylvia, "You should write a book." With that she answered, "I have," She explained how she began writing the book in the year 2000, after Tony's death.

It had been sitting in the drawer now for seven years. She explained to John that she hadn't done anything with it because it was an autobiography, and she didn't like saying, "I did this." or "I did that."

She then turned to John, and asked, "John would you change the book into third person form for me?" He replied, "I'll think about it." That day, when he went home to his wife, he told her what Sylvia had asked him to do. He asked her what she thought of the idea. She encouraged him, and suggested he take on the challenge.

The next time John went to Sylvia's office, he told her, "My wife told me to take the job." Sylvia quickly pulled out the whole manuscript and gave him all she had done of it. Sylvia then wrote another few chapters to bring it up to date.

John, worked diligently at the task set before him. Every so often he would bring what he had done of it for her approval. Often, he would do some research, to clarify things that she wrote. This process took approximately three to four months.

At the time, Sylvia wanted the title to be "Till the End of Time." However, John felt that ultimately, it was a story about how Sylvia's Haven came to be, and suggested they rename it "Sylvia's Haven," Sylvia agreed.

After John had completed his task, he then asked Sylvia, "Who should we have publish the book?" Sylvia replied, "I don't know, you are good on the computer, make a search and see what you come up with."

John did exactly as Sylvia asked, and found a publisher who, ironically, was at a convention featuring companies of that nature, in Boston. John suggested that he and Sylvia go and see what they had to offer. Sylvia agreed.

When they arrived, the representatives for the publisher painted a very rosy picture of their company. John and Sylvia, being unfamiliar with the whole process, bought it.

When Sylvia sent in the manuscript, she got the first run for her approval. She was not too pleased with the results, called the company and made arrangements to go to the company and talk to them personally. She felt that if she showed them the exactly what she wanted, everything would turn out fine.

What she didn't know was, they did not do the printing in house. The actual printing of the book was farmed out to another printer. Therefore, all the time and expense to go to the office of the publisher, was a waste of time and money.

Each time, the current printed copy of the book was sent to Sylvia, for examination, Sylvia would make the necessary corrections and send it back. This went on for 10 times. By this time, Sylvia was at her wits end.

She gave specific orders on how the cover should be. She actually designed the book cover herself. When the cover was completed, it was sent to her for approval. By this time, she was so anxious to get the book on the road, that at first glance, it looked fine. She approved the cover, and the book went to print.

She purchased 250 hard covers, and 250 paper backs. The publishing company gave her, as a bonus, 25 hard covers and 25 paper backs. The cost of printing was very costly, naturally, because they had to pay for the printing and still make a profit. The royalties were also lower than others.

They promised to send out press releases. Sylvia received the copies of the releases. They sent her about 1000 of them, from every one horse town they could find, all worthless.

Sylvia, before the book was published, called her pastor and asked for an appointment to see him. A time was set, and on the appointed time went to his office. She informed him that she was writing a book and wanted his opinion in a particular portion of the book, before it was published. He graciously gave his opinion.

When the books were delivered, Sylvia went right to her pastor and gave him the first copy. He suggested that she bring some of the books with her the following Sunday. The pastor told her he would have a table set up in the lobby for the sale of the books.

That Sunday, the pastor, announced from the pulpit that Sylvia had written a book, and they would be for sale in the lobby after services. It was amazing to Sylvia to see the response. She was very grateful to her pastor for being so gracious.

Chapter 32

About mid-August 2007, Sylvia thought she might be coming down with a virus of some sort. She had been studying nutrition for twenty years, and took a variety of supplements. Every time she started to feel like the flu was coming on, she'd take oscillo, a homeopathic medicine. It had worked for her every time before, but not this time.

One evening, she began having a very bad breathing problem, she was hyperventilating and becoming frightened. If this episode didn't stop soon, she would have to call 911. Shortly after she made that decision, it did stop. A shortness of breath, however, continued. It was difficult for her to climb stairs, stopping every third step to recover. Lifting large or heavy bundles was out of the question.

After about five and a half weeks of going through this, Sylvia finally conceded that it was nothing ordinary, and she needed to get some professional help. She called the New England Baptist Hospital, where she had her cancer surgery in June 1990. Through their physician referral service, she contacted a doctor who wanted her to get some tests right away, based on what Sylvia had relayed through a receptionist. The doctor was not only concerned about the symptoms, but the fact that she was seventy-seven years old didn't help.

On October 3, Jim took her to the hospital. He was a bit upset that a wheelchair wasn't offered. As she walked along the corridor she had to stop every ten feet to catch her breath. In any case, she was seen quickly. The triage nurse took her vitals, and when she timed her heart, it was beating at a dangerous 157 beats per minute. The nurse hollered for help, and people started coming out of the woodwork.

The doctor arrived and injected her with something to bring her heart rate down. He explained that she was going to have a reaction to the medicine. He injected her again, but still no reaction. After the third injection, she started hyperventilating again. It was the reaction the doctor was looking for, and her heart rate went down to eighty-eight. When things calmed down, she asked the doctor what was normal, and was told that sixty or seventy was a good range.

Sylvia was admitted with what was termed congestive heart failure. The doctor told Jim she would be staying for two or three days. After two of those days, it would be Sylvia's seventy-eighth birthday. But on that October fifth, she was not alone. Cards, flowers, and friends were with her.

Her stay ended up being six days. On the day before her discharge, a Sunday, her doctor entered her room and announced that she had done it. Her body had reverted back to a normal rhythm that morning, and she was going to be all right. Sylvia knew she had done nothing. God had stepped in again on her behalf. As she was leaving the hospital, she was given five prescriptions and an appointment to be seen in about a week.

She went back to work, although took life a bit slower. Jim noticed the difference immediately. Some of her old dynamic energy was back, and strikingly better than the weeks prior to her hospital stay.

She resumed making last minute preparations for a banquet celebrating the twentieth anniversary of Sylvia's Haven. She was so grateful to God for keeping her well enough to see the banquet come to fruition. It was an opulent and beautiful time of fellowship for all who attended. Her dream was fulfilled.

The next week, she kept her doctor's appointment and everything seemed well. The doctor scheduled another appointment for the second week in November for an echocardiogram. About two days before that appointment however, she felt unusually listless. When she arrived at the doctor's office two days later, a technician began the echo. At one point, she raised the volume so high Sylvia could hear the pulses. It sounded like a loud drum beat, banging at a very rapid pace. Sylvia asked the technician what the sound was. She answered, "Your heart!"

Her heart was beating 150 times per minute, and the doctor was called by cell phone to report the dilemma. He appeared shortly thereafter and admitted her back into the hospital. This time, the doctor tried a new medication. He told Sylvia that, with this new medication, the manufacturer insisted the patient stay in the hospital for three days and be carefully observed; there was a one percent chance of a reaction.

The first day went well. On the second day, she felt a slight numbness on the right side of her face and noticed white circles in her vision. While concerned, the episode lasted for just a few minutes and was gone. She said nothing to the nurses or doctor.

On the third day, Sylvia's sister was visiting, when all of a sudden, Sylvia started gasping for breath and her heart stopped beating. She tried to climb out of the bed and passed out falling face down onto the floor. Her sister panicked and, as she was leaving the room to get help, she saw doctors, nurses, even security guards rushing to the room.

They kept telling her sister to wait in the lounge but she would have none of it. Her sister later related how the staff kept yelling Sylvia's name as they tried to revive her. She had flat-lined, she was dead for fifteen minutes. Then, a nurse decided to turn her on her back and lift her head. Suddenly, she opened her eyes and wondered how she had gotten on the floor and was a bit amazed at all of the people around her. God had once again intervened. What an awesome God!

The doctor ordered that medication stopped and another was ordered instead. After a total stay of five days, and stabilized, she was sent home with instructions to take her pulse every morning and evening. She told them she did not know how. Sylvia is the type of person who, when interested in a subject, will make every effort to find out all she can. But, if there was no need to learn, she just let it be.

Now there was a reason to learn and, once home, a visiting nurse showed her how to take her pulse. Her daughter-in-law, being a nurse, said she would buy her an instrument as an early Christmas present. Attached to her wrist, it would take her pulse and blood pressure for her. It took only three days for her son to call and tell her they had the device and asked her to come and get it. Sylvia faithfully took her blood pressure and pulse every morning and every night from then on.

About a week later, she began feeling very sluggish. One morning, when she took her pulse, she noted that it was up to 160. Sylvia was alarmed but decided to wait fifteen minutes and test again. She did so and it registered at 125. Thinking this was a temporary episode, she waited another fifteen minutes, tested again, but this time it was back up to 160.

She called the doctor's office, and told them of her findings. Her doctor was contacted by phone and told his office to get her into the hospital. Sylvia drove herself there and, again, everyone went to work on her. She was again hooked up to an automatic blood pressure machine that took her pressure repeatedly.

At first, it was every five minutes, later, every fifteen. They made preparations to admit her once again. As soon as a room was ready, they began medicating her and regularly took her vital signs. They watched her in this manner for four days, but her pulse remained irregular.

On the fourth day, her doctor visited again and told her that, since her heart had not gone back to a normal rhythm with the medication, he would like to perform a cardioversion (the application of an electric shock to restore a regular heart beat). She gave permission.

The next day she was anaesthetized and the procedure completed. They kept her in the ICU for four hours, watching her closely. The procedure was a success and her heartbeat was now, in it's normal rhythm. She was sent home on the fifth day, about a week and a half before Christmas of 2007.

With the help of her sister, Sylvia prepared her usual Christmas dinner and yet there was something very special about this season. She was very thankful to be alive, and she gives God all the glory.

Chapter 33

On New Year's Eve, Sylvia purchased some Chinese food and took it home to share with Stephanie and her children.

On January 3, 2008, Sylvia received a call from a yet another homeless girl. Referred to Sylvia by "A Woman's Concern", Sylvia set up an appointment for the following day. Madeline has a four-year-old daughter and is expecting a baby girl in March. She moved in on January 5, 2008.

Sylvia thought this would be an excellent match. Vera, turning four in March, now has a playmate. When Madeline has her baby, in a few months, the baby will be able to play with Anton. Everything seems to be working out well.

This addition to Sylvia's Haven became yet another and still growing milestone. Madeline and her daughter are charges counted as 999 and 1000. And, on February 24, 2008, one woman was accepted, making precisely one thousand and one women and children, seeking, accepted and assisted by Sylvia's Haven.

Sylvia then was instructed to go to the doctor's office on a regular basis so that she could be closely mornitored. She did everything they directed her to do.

She often wondered how, when she flat-lined she was on her back, when the nurse lifted her head. On one of the visits to the doctor's office, a nurse approached her and told her she was present when she flat-lined. Sylvia, asked her, "How come I was on my back when I opened my eyes, I know from the way I was trying to get out of bed that I had to have been face down?" She replied, "I turned you over and lifted your head." Sylvia is sure God instructed the nurse on what to do.

Sylvia noted that in many cases she had read about after death experiences, there was a light at the end of a tunnel, and a beautiful vision of heaven. The other examples she heard of was the opposite, when the hounds of hell came to bring the lost soul to hell.

In Sylvia's case, neither of these episodes occurred, there was nothing. Sylvia feels, it was because God had no intention of taking her then.

For the next two years, she continued her regular visits to the doctor. However, with the medication alone there was no solution to the problem. She honestly felt it was a gradual down-hill experience, and knew she needed another doctor.

One day, she received a call from a woman who wanted to volunteer her services. She asked what she could do to help. Sylvia told her that what she really needed was help addressing plea letters. These were letters sent out to people not familiar with Sylvia's Haven. The names were simply taken from the telephone book, with the hope of reaching anyone who might be interested to help.

As she spoke, it became evident that she lived quite a distance away. She also said she had about twelve women willing to help. She said she would come and pick the material up and bring it home, so that everyone could work at it from there home base.

Sylvia then asked, "Where do you live?" She replied, "Littleton." This town was located very close to Devens, and she had wanted to go there to see her friends, that she had breakfast with every morning while she was at Devens.

She then told her, she needn't come all the way over to Revere, that she would go there and give her the material she needed. This gave Sylvia the excuse she wanted to see her friends. She told her to meet her at Johnson's Restaurant at 10:00 A.M. on Wednesday. (This is where Sylvia ate with her friends every morning.)

On Wednesday, when Sylvia arrived, the woman was at Johnson's, waiting for her. She gave her the work and instructions. The woman told her she would have the material ready for her in one week.

Sylvia went inside the restaurant and ordered her food. The workers were surprised to see her. She sat down and not long after, one of the four couples she ate with, came in. They had a very pleasant reunion together, the others did not show.

When she was about to leave she asked Claire if she would call the other three couples, and tell them she would return next week and would like to see them. When she returned the following week, the volunteer had finished the work and handed it to her. Sylvia was very grateful and thanked her.

She then went into the restaurant and three of the four couples were anxiously waiting for her. Everyone was so happy to see her and Sylvia was just as happy to see them. They explained that the fourth couple had a doctor's appointment and could not be there. Then the husband of one of the couples asked Sylvia what was the exact problem with her heart, because each one of them received her newsletter regularly, and in them she hinted she was having a problem.

Sylvia explained the symptoms, how her heart would race and told them the whole story as we mentioned earlier. At that point, he asked, "Sylvia, did you ever think of getting another doctor?" Sylvia replied, "Yes, many times, I just don't know who to go to." With that he said, "I had the same problem you're having, and I have the best doctor there is for that problem. He did a procedure where they inserted tubes to my heart, he was on a computer, and fixed the problem. I've been well now for four years."

Sylvia asked him if he would give her the name of the doctor. He said, "I have his name and number in my car, I'll be right back." He came back with all the information she needed.

They all chattered for a while and left. Sylvia went back to work, and vowed the next time she got another attack, she would get in touch with this doctor. About a month later, sure enough, the problem reoccurred.

She called the doctor's office, and the receptionist answered. Sylvia explained her problem, and asked for an appointment. The receptionist told her that there wasn't an opening for three months. Sylvia said, "I can't wait that long, my heart is beating at 150 beats a minute, now. I need help right away." With that she said she would talk to the doctor's nurse, and to hold on. His nurse came to the phone, and Sylvia repeated what she had told the receptionist. The nurse said "the earliest we can take you is two weeks." Sylvia, wasn't happy with the answer, but made the appointment anyway.

She thought to herself, I hope I can make it but if matters get worse I will have to go back to my doctor. A few hours later, she received another call from the doctor's nurse. This time she said she spoke to the doctor and he told her to call Sylvia back, and tell her that he would fit her in at 9:00 A.M., Wednesday morning, this was on a Monday. Sylvia assured her that she would be there.

Wednesday morning, Sylvia was there promptly at 9:00 A.M. When she met the doctor, she told him that he came highly recommended by one of his patients who had the same problem. She said he told her that since the procedure, he has been well for four years.

He ordered some tests taken, and after seeing the results, he told her, that indeed, she did have the same problem. He told her he would do the procedure for her, but he wanted to have a blood test, because she was taking Coumadin, and normally they could not operate until she was off of the Coumadin for five full days.

However, he was anxious to get started before the results had come back and told her to eat a lot of green leafy vegetables, he said, that would thicken the blood faster. When the blood results came back they realized that it would be dangerous to proceed before the full five days, and postponed the procedure for another week.

Chapter 34

On Friday at 2:00 P.M., she was present at the hospital for the procedure. She asked the doctor, what they called this procedure. He told her it was called an oblation. They prepared Sylvia for the procedure and administered a liquid anesthesia intravenously, among other things.

They inserted the tubes from her groin to her heart. The doctor sat away from her and had a screen, where he manned all of the controls to do the procedure. On the screen he could see clearly where the problems were and there were many.

One at a time, very carefully, he handled each problem. Sylvia was awake through most of the procedure. She could feel very slightly, each time he took care of a problem. At one point, he had to work harder to rectify the problem, and Sylvia could feel the extra pressure.

With this the doctor, who was very caring, left his seat, and came over to Sylvia and asked, "On a scale of one to ten how much pressure did you feel?" she replied, "Eight." At this point, he must have instructed the anesthetist to administer a little more anesthesia. With this, Sylvia fell asleep.

The procedure must have taken a total of two and a half to three hours, as near as Sylvia could figure out. When the doctor was through, he approached Sylvia, that since it was so late, he thought it would be best to keep her at the hospital overnight.

Normally, after a few hours rest, the patient would be sent home. But it was now after 5:00 P.M. and he thought his decision was a wise one. The next day, Sylvia was released.

The procedure was a success. Sylvia gradually began to improve. Before this time, when she was feeling so sick with no end in sight. She didn't even think of going any further with Sylvia's Haven, she had all she could do to operate the one house she had.

As she began to feel better she wanted desperately, to have the book "Sylvia's Haven" be a success. The publisher of "Sylvia's Haven" called her, and told her that there was a company who had a magazine that catered to authors who wished to reach TV and Radio shows for interviews to publicize their book. This magazine went out only to TV stations and Radio stations that were interested in having authors as guests on their show.

She would have to purchase ads to be put in this magazine at an exorbitant cost. Since Sylvia had such a bad experience with this publisher, she quickly declined the offer.

That evening as she thought about it, she remembered being told that all of the help were inexperienced and were only taught how to do only one thing. In this case, they were taught the pitch and nothing more. She called back the next day, and asked for the person that had contacted her the day before.

She asked that person, what was the name of the publication, and the name of the company who published the publication. They readily told her the name of the publication was "Radio-TV Interview Report," the company was Bradley Communications, Corp.

Sylvia called the Company and ordered half page ads at nearly half the price. During this time she was told that they had seminars to help in marketing her book. She attended the seminars. Steve and Bill Harrison and the whole staff at Bradley Communications have been very helpful to her. She has learned a lot from them. They have bent over backwards to be of help to her, in many ways.

She even met a woman on their staff who informed her that she had experience in turning books into screen plays and she thought "Sylvia's Haven" would make a great movie. She offered to do this for her. Sylvia highly recommends them to everyone who asks about their integrity, honesty and genuine interest in seeing that their clients are well instructed.

Soon another company contacted Sylvia to go to their seminar, much like the one Bradley Communications was presenting. The price was right and Sylvia was eager to learn as much as she could possibly learn about marketing her book. These seminars were run by Brendon Burchard. It was the practice in both of these seminars, that at the beginning of the sessions, they would ask each person to introduce themselves, what company they represented and what was their interest in attending the seminar.

In this particular seminar, when Sylvia was called on to introduce herself, she did as she did at the Bradley Communication's Seminar. She gave her name and explained that her company was a shelter for homeless women and children, and that she had written a book called "Sylvia's Haven."

However, this time she went one step further and asked if there was anyone there who could help her update her website. She explained she was a woman who was eighty-one years of age and not too computer literate and needed help in this area. One young gentleman, Venu Sripada, offered to help and to this day helps her whenever she needs help. He has done an excellent job. There was another man there who put her on You Tube. Everyone was so helpful. Brendan is another she would highly recommend for his sincerity, honesty and willingness to go the extra mile to help.

One day Sylvia received a call from Venu, the young gentleman who offered to bring her web site up to date. He asked her if she went to many seminars. She stated so far only two different ones. He informed her he was going to attend a different one and was going to be a volunteer helper at this seminar, and because of his volunteering he could invite someone to attend at a discounted rate. He asked Sylvia if she would like to attend this seminar, he praised it so highly, Sylvia accepted the offer. Little did she know what she was getting into.

Chapter 35

She paid the discounted rate and made arrangements, with his help to attend the meeting. The first session was to begin at 1:00 P.M. However, Venu suggested that she get there early, because although the section she was to be in was arranged, the seats were not guaranteed. It was on a first come first served basis. The title of the seminar was "Unleash the Power Within," or UPW, by Tony Robbins. Up to this point Sylvia had never heard of Tony Robbins.

The doors opened at 9:00 A.M. Sylvia made sure she was there as soon as the door opened. She was expecting to see about 110 to 125 people at the auditorium, similar to the last two she went to. Lo and behold, there were thousands of people there, four thousand to be exact. The lobby was packed. All she could think of was, she was going to have to stand for four hours until they allowed the people to enter the area where the seminar was to be held.

At this particular time, she had been having heart problems for a little over two years. She was on medication but in the past, it had been gradual downhill slide. Even though she had this new procedure, down deep inside she still had her fears. She felt she could never endure standing on her feet for four hours.

Sylvia began looking around for the possibility of finding someplace to sit. She soon found a very small meeting room that probably sat about two hundred people. There was a young fellow near the door and she asked him if she could sit there. He told her it was quite alright.

Sylvia quickly sat down. About ten minutes later, a woman came up to Sylvia and said, "You can't sit here, this area is reserved for the help only." Sylvia quietly got up and left the room. She stood outside that room for about another ten minutes, and the woman must have had second thoughts. She approached Sylvia, and told her she had put two chairs outside the small auditorium for people with special needs.

Sylvia never thought of herself as being special needs. However, she sat down quickly, and was very appreciative of the change of heart. After some time, Sylvia decided to get up and move around. There were many booths to look at and she stopped at one that had the heading "Coaching."

She spoke to a gentleman, at the booth named James Cunnings. They talked for quite some time together. Sylvia signed up for six months of coaching sessions. She also mentioned how the woman gave her a seat and dubbed her "special needs."

James told her, since she was now labeled special needs she could go right up in front of the crowd and could sit wherever she wanted. James, not only was of help to Sylvia that day but to this day continues to be of great help to her. Sylvia has found a great friend in James that she will be ever grateful to God for, he is a gift from heaven.

At this point, it was nearly 1:00 P.M. and the doors were about to open. Sylvia quickly got to the door and explained she was special needs. The guards at the door positioned her second in line. Only one other woman was before her. The woman was escorted to the front of the auditorium, and she chose to sit on the right side of the stage. Sylvia's escort chose to sit her where he thought best, it was about eight rows back, in front of the stage on the aisle seat. She was grateful to be that close.

She really had no idea as to what to expect. She soon found out the sessions were real long, from 1:00 P.M. to 10:00 P.M. Now mind you this woman was afraid to do very much because of her heart problem. She loved to dance, but thought to herself she would never be able to dance again, except for perhaps one or two very slow dances.

Tony Robbins likes to keep his audience active. For one thing he does not like them to sit. He also realizes if they are to be there for 10 hours of more, they must stay active. Therefore, he would have them dancing, from time to time as they were standing. Occasionally, he would have them do some exercising, and from time to time he would have each row turn to the right and then to the left and each person would message the back of the person in front of them. This was totally new to Sylvia.

What's more, she danced all day, let alone stand on her feet for ten hours. At the end of the first day, if a person wanted to participate, they had coals burning outside the building all day. When the flame had gone out but the coals were still hot, between 1200 and 2000 degrees farenheit, they could go out and walk on the hot coals. Everyone close to Sylvia asked her if she was going to walk on the hot coals. She simply replied, I'm going out there and see what happens, if the others can do it, I can do it to. That evening when it came time to end the session the last thing to do was to go out and walk on those very hot coals.

Sylvia got in line and watched until she found herself in front of the hot coals. There was nothing left to do but to go out and walk, and walk she did. Proving, "What the mind can conceive and believe it can achieve," as Napoleon Hill states. Tony Robbins states, "Once you start doing the impossible (or at least what you thought was impossible), you can conquer the other fires of your life with ease." This seminar was to last four days, from November 4, 2010 to November 7, 2010, in New Jersey.

The second day, she became sort of overly confident. Because she was special needs she felt she didn't have to rush. Much to her surprise the seat she wanted was taken and she ended up in the middle of the auditorium. The third day she made sure she got there early enough so that she would be the first in line. She chose the first row on the right hand side of the stage, about the third seat in. Now she was only about 8 feet away from Tony, except he was high on a platform that was perhaps seven feet above the floor.

She danced and danced all day. At one point Tony came to the edge of the stage and beckoned to Sylvia and said, "Come here." Sylvia walked up to the edge of the stage and Tony bent down, and asked, "How old are you?" Sylvia replied, "Eighty-one years old. Tony then asked, "What's your name?" Sylvia replied, "Sylvia Anthony."

Sylvia then said to him, "I would like to talk to you, I run a home for homeless women and children and I wrote a book." There was loud music playing in the background and Tony replied, "I can't hear you," then pointing to a guard standing beside me, he said, "You tell him what you want to say and he will tell me." Then he straightened out and yelled to the crowd, "Give Sylvia a big hand."

All of the 4000 people clapped and cheered. Sylvia was shocked. Sylvia had taken ten copies of her first book "Sylvia's Haven," to give or to sell to people interested in having a book. If she had 4000 of them she could have sold them all. She then turned to the guard as instructed and repeated what she told Tony. That she ran a home for homeless women and children and had written a book. The guard asked, "Do you have a book here?" She had already given out 3 of the 10 books, and she replied, "Yes." He said, "Give me one and I will see that Tony gets it."

Sylvia went back to her seat and took a book and gave it to the guard. Then she said, "I also want to talk to Tony." He nodded, yes, as though that could be arranged. What Sylvia didn't realize was that Tony was not going to appear in person the next day, he would appear via video tape.

When Sylvia returned to her seat and went out for a break, she sold the remainder of the books in a matter of a few minutes. People were coming up to ask to have their picture taken with her, and some even handed her a donation. She gave out many cards and received many. This went on for the remainder of the two days, she felt like a celebrity.

On the fourth and final day, she took a seat in the front row in front of the stage. She left her seat before the start of the seminar to get a drink. When she returned one of the guards was waiting for her. He approached her with a card, about the size of an index card. He told her that in the afternoon there was to be a dance party.

He then told her that Tony was very impressed with her and had taken an interest in her. He wanted her to appear on stage for a solo during the dance party. When the party started, she was told to give this card to the guards. This card was her identification card for permission to enter the stage.

When the time came, Sylvia didn't have to show the card to the guards, and there were about six of them all around the stage. They all knew who she was, and beckoned to her to get set to go on stage. They pointed to the right hand side of the stage where there was a young lady waiting for her, who was to give her the cue as to when to enter the stage.

It took all morning and half of the afternoon for her to realize that Tony was not going to be there that day. Sylvia went to the guard who she gave the book to and asked if Tony was going to be there, and of course he told her it was his day off. Then she said, "I wanted to speak to him." He told her to write everything she wanted to say down and give it to him and he would see to it that Tony got the letter.

She went back to the young lady and asked her for some paper and a pen so that she could write to Tony. She came back with a piece of paper about the size of the index card. Sylvia explained, "I need a sheet of about 8 ½ x 11." She quickly returned with a full size sheet. Sylvia wrote all she wanted to write. About what she does for a living and about the book she wrote, which she already gave to the guard to give to him.

Now, she was signaled to go on stage and dance a solo, it was meant to be something everyone in the audience to copy and dance right along with her. Since she had been a dance instructor in her early twenties, this was no problem and the audience followed right along. After she was through, she again got a resounding ovation. Sylvia had danced for four days straight. Nine hours the first day and thirteen hours, off and on, each day for the next three days. A feat she would have never thought possible. She will never forget those four days as long as she lives.

In the beginning of December, Sylvia got an E-Mail from the Tony Robbins' office inviting her to a "Date with Destiny," DWD, as his guest and could she make it. She sent an E-Mail back immediately, stating, "Yes, yes, yes." It was to be at Palm Springs, California. This was just about 2 weeks before the event. She was only asked to purchase some material needed before the event, at a very nominal cost. She quickly made the airplane and hotel reservations close to the auditorium.

Sylvia was very grateful to Tony for extending the invitation. To quote Tony Robbins, a Date with Destiny, "Át its core, this program is about understanding why you feel and behave the way you do as well as giving you strategies and tools that will allow you to align with these forces to create happiness, joy, love, passion, success, and fulfillment you desire and deserve." When Sylvia arrived at the auditorium, she quickly looked for the person or persons in charge of seating. She found a woman who assigned her a section, as she would routinely, and gave Sylvia a name tag with the section on it to be worn around her neck. Sylvia never questioned the assignment. She took it and thanked her and proceeded to find the location of the section she was assigned to.

She was there for about fifteen minutes, when a man came up to Sylvia he told her she had the wrong seating assignment, gave her the new name tag, and took back the old one. He also escorted her to her new assignment. She was assigned to Team No.1. This was the elite group, and Tony Robbins put her there. They were assigned a section closest to the left side of the stage. She was told that everyone in this group must have a partner, and a young lady offered to be her partner. Sylvia was seated in the first row first seat with her partner beside her. Again, she was made to feel like a queen.

Each day had a new theme. The third day had to do with relationship and what love should be all about. Tony, gave an example of the difference between man and woman that was very unique, to Sylvia's eyes. He held up a very thin man's wallet and said, "Just to show you how different women are, this is all that a man carries with him." He opened the wallet and showed some money, identification and some credit cards. Then he picked up a woman's large size handbag, and said, "This is what a woman carries with her." He began to pull out only a small portion of what was in it to make his point.

The point being made is that women are different than men. They require understanding, love and attention. This to Sylvia was very logical, after all isn't that what anyone wants male or female? Then Tony asked for two volunteers. He said he wanted two women to depict what the sex act should be like. Sylvia, raised her hand. Tony saw Sylvia's hand had go up and said, "Sylvia, come here."

Now, Sylvia was sorry she ever raised her hand. Fear gripped her for a moment and she quickly prayed to God. "Dear God, please help me, I don't want this demonstration to be cheapening. I want it to show that sex should be a total commitment between two people who love each other and live only for one another, as you intended it to be."

Suddenly, Sylvia and three others emerged on the stage. Tony said, "I only asked for two." However, Tony asked for two more chairs and kept them on the stage. He had the theme from "Ghost" playing and asked them to show what they thought sex should be like.

They played only about two lines of the song and stopped and asked the audience to give there applause after each person was pointed out. Two were quickly eliminated. Then Sylvia's partner called out to Tony complaining that the third girl never even moved. Tony told the young lady to come sit next to Sylvia and watch what Sylvia was doing and follow her. This time the song was played from beginning to end.

Sylvia moved very slowly to the rhythm of the music, her hands oustretched, and moving, as if praying to God. When the music was over, the audience gave a resounding applause for Sylvia's interpretation. Tony, hugged Sylvia, and whispered, "You were the best."

Whenever, Sylvia left the auditorium for a snack or break, people would go up to her and congratulate her on her performance. She would explain the message she was trying to portray was a pure total love and commitment. Everyone said that is the exact message they got. Sylvia was pleased with the outcome. Many of the people asked to have pictures taken with her. It again, was a very memorable occasion for Sylvia.

The following month, January 2011, Sylvia received an E-Mail from a gentleman who told her he saw her at "A Date With Destiny," and had signed up for Business Mastery, another of Tony's seminars. He said he signed up for it at the end of that session, and that if a person did sign up, they could bring a guest free of charge. He asked Sylvia, Would you like to come along as my guest? If so, I will inform the office and give them your name as my guest." Sylvia graciously accepted.

Business Mastery, teaches the importance of keeping abreast of the financial status of your company, as well as many aspects of running a successful business. Sylvia learned a lot from this session and was so very grateful for being invited. Many of the people there had been to the other two sessions and it was like meeting old friends all over again.

Chapter 36

When the seminar was over Sylvia returned to work and worked diligently to catch up with all the work that was waiting for her. Things were very bad financially and she had to lay herself and her assistant Jim off in order to cut expenses. She worked as a volunteer without pay and Jim donated two days a week as a volunteer.

Things got worse. Jim's parents were old and ailing and Jim had to be the one to take care of them. God has a way of providing for everything, because if he hadn't had a layoff, he would not have been able to take care of his parents. This left Sylvia to do 95% of the work with no help and no funds to pay anyone.

Sylvia struggled desperately to keep her head above water. This was nothing new for Sylvia because many times during the nearly 25 years she was in a financial crunch. When she started Life for the Little Ones, Inc., She loaned $20,000.00 to the new non-profit to get it off the ground, and worked free of charge from 1987 to the end of 1993.

Then gradually with the Boards permission they stated she should receive $30,000.00 per year. But as stated previously, they stated when the money was available. The problem then was that they were only grossing $30,000.00 per year. Therefore, she simply took what she could of the expense money she had given to the company as a loan, when- ever possible.

Another bad crunch came when the law suit at Devens was underway and the smear campaign began that nearly broke the back of Sylvia's Haven. God always protected Sylvia and the shelter and somehow always came out of the adversity a stronger person for it.

Now she was in another one of these seemingly insurmountable problems. Undaunted, she persevered. This is now an ongoing problem. There was some respite, however. When things were in a better financial status, about eight years before, she bought and paid for a timeshare in Hawaii. Each year she would book her vacation about one year in advance.

This year the vacation was set for March 20, 2011 to April 3, 2011. All she had to have was her airfare and money for expenses that she was saving for all year long. By this time she was long overdue for a rest and took it gladly. It was the most beautiful and restful vacation she ever had. She scheduled her time the first week to see a few sights. She went to a dance class one day, and a play, "Driving Miss Daisy," one night and one day she did a little window shopping at a beautiful mall in Maui.

The rest of this vacation was spent just relaxing. The back of the building she owed sat on the sand of the beach and when she lied down from her bed she could see the ocean and sky. She took a laptop with her and between resting and eating and making a lei, she completed about four chapters of this book. She will always thank God for this rest she needed so badly. It was truly a gift from God.

Jim met Sylvia at the airport and brought her to work and on the way briefed her on what went on while she was away. One of the things he said in passing was, "Your cousin called, I believe her name is Tina." When they arrived at the office he gave her the telephone number of the woman who had called.

It turned out that it was not Tina that called, but her niece Carolyn. When Sylvia called her, she told her that her aunt Tina was seriously ill. She said, "I know you would want to know because Tina spoke of you often. She told her Tina had cancer of the pancreas. Sylvia asked her what hospital she was in, because Sylvia loved Tina dearly. As mentioned earlier Tina babysat Sylvia and they were very close.

That evening Jim went back to Groton to take care of his parents. The next day he called Sylvia to tell her his mother had passed away. She asked him to let her know when the services would be, and that she wanted to attend. He said he would inform her as soon as he knew. When she was told she went to the funeral home and gave her condolences, to Jim, his father and the rest of the family. Needless to say, Jim had his hands full.

Sylvia went to see Tina at the hospital, her oldest son, Frank was there. She hadn't seen him since he was a baby of about two years old, he was now sixty-three. Tina perked right up when she saw Sylvia and told her the illness came on quite suddenly. She started getting stomach pains in February.

Before that she fell between an electronic door. Somehow, she was healed of that, and told Sylvia she kept herself very active donating her time at the store on the senior citizen complex she was living in. Prior to that, she was the Secretary on the Board of the complex. She was always active and well-liked by all.

At one point, during her first visit, Tina asked, "Sylvia, if I tell you something will you believe me?" She assured her she would. Tina said, "There's a little girl here I see her and she shaking all over as though she is afraid for something." Tina was Catholic. Sylvia asked, Tina have you seen a priest. Tina replied, "Sylvia, I have a lot of people praying for me."

Sylvia then said, "Tina it is very nice that you have a lot of people praying for you, but you have to talk to God. God wants you to talk to Him. You have to tell him that you are sorry for any sins you may have committed, and tell God that you want to turn your life over to him." She continued, "Think back at all of the times in your life that God has helped you, I'm sure there are many times that He did." Tina replied, "Oh yes," and she began to innumerate some examples. Then Tina said, "I have to put myself in God's hands and tell him I'm sorry for my sins," and Sylvia replied, "Yes."

Then Tina said, "Sylvia, that little girl is back, she's here." She pointed to a spot beside her bed between Tina and Sylvia. The she said, She is stroking my arm." She showed Sylvia how she was stroking her arm, repeatedly and gently as if to calm her. It was as if the girl had nothing more to fear, Tina would be with the Lord.

Sylvia continued to see Tina about every other day. The next time she went her son Frank and Jimmy were there. She was then informed that Tina's condition had become worse. The cancer had spread to the liver. At this point, she had little or no appetite left and found it very hard to swallow. Her sons pleaded with her to eat, but it was as if they didn't want to face the reality that their mother wasn't going to get better.

She was now eighty-eight years of age. Sylvia thought it very significant, that she wanted to look very nice for Sylvia, and asked her sons to bring her some of her better dresses to wear at the hospital. At one point, Sylvia asked Tina if she saw the little girl anymore and she said, "No."

The next time Sylvia went to see Tina, again some of her sons were there. Tina had four sons. In a short period of time Sylvia got to know her sons as though no time had elapsed. At this point, Tina implied that maybe she was sick because God was punishing her. Sylvia replied, "God loves you. He loves you so much He wants to take you home with him, so that you will never have to suffer again. You will have a whole new body that will never decay." That seemed to reassure her and she seemed more at peace.

As time went on Tina became less and less lucid. They now had her on morphine. One evening Sylvia went to see Tina much later than usual. It was after 7:00 P.M. When she went into her room, she noticed that Tina was heavily sedated. What's more she sensed that would be the last time she would see Tina alive.

The next day, Tina's son Frank, called Sylvia and informed her, his mother had passed away. Then in the next breath he said, "The four of us had a meeting," meaning Tina's four sons, "and we all agreed, that we would like to have you say the eulogy, we know our mother would want that." Sylvia felt so honored and humbled by this gesture, that she quickly replied, "I certainly will, I would consider it an honor and a privilege." The church service was on Good Friday, and Sylvia noted, what an honor God had bestowed on Tina having her service on Good Friday, the same day Jesus died.

Sylvia went to church one Sunday, and the sermon Pastor Rick preached seemed so apropos at this particular time. She asked her Pastor if he would give her permission to include it in the last chapter and last paragraph of her book. He gladly consented. It reads as follows:-

"Our story is a part of God's larger story, and in God's story there are no minor characters. In God's story we all matter regardless of how large our role may seem in the eyes of other people. In God's story everyone has value and importance.

Jeremiah 49:11 says, "But I will protect the orphans who remain among you. Your widows, too, can depend on me for help."

Elsewhere God instructs landowners to leave the edges of their fields un-harvested so that the poor and widows can come and gather enough food to eat. In these instances God, the great Author of the story, is saying these people who society might have a tendency to overlook will not be overlooked by me, the people that others might be tempted to forget God remembers. They may not be landowners, politicians, wealthy, or even employed, but they are important people in God's story and so they must be important people to us as well.

As we live our lives, the same societal troubles persist for some. From the beginning of time, a father, a mother, a husband, a friend might not always have become what God intended. They all have free choices in their lives. But the children and their mothers must always be able to find help when help is needed. Sylvia's Haven, is there.

Nearly twenty-five years ago, Sylvia had a dream. She still has that dream and God in her heart. As for the homeless women, single, abused, with or without children those with little hope, Sylvia's Haven will never quit. With God's divine intervention and guidance, with continued support from her board, contributors, and staff, Sylvia's Haven will be there, offering a helping hand when none existed before.

A WORD FROM THE AUTHOR

I wish to thank you from the very bottom of my heart and soul, for the valuable time you have taken, to read this book.

As you can readily see, The Haven cannot exist, much less grow, without your help. Your help is greatly appreciated, it is a way of giving back that makes a world of difference.

May God continue to richly bless you, and all your loved ones.

I hope you have enjoyed this book!

www.sylviashaven.org E-Mail sylviashaveninc@aol.com
Sylvia Anthony
Sylvia's Haven
7 Foster St., Suite 29
Revere, MA 02151
Tel. 781-629-4327

All donations are tax deductible. A sincere thank you note will be sent for your tax records.

CPSIA information can be obtained at www.ICGtesting.com
Printed in the USA
BVOW082308090212

282608BV00002B/1/P